Sweet Influences
of the Anointing

Second Edition

DAG HEWARD-MILLS

Parchment House

Unless otherwise stated, all Scripture quotations are taken from the
King James Version of the Bible

First published 2013 by Parchment House
15th Printing 2018

[77]Find out more about Dag Heward-Mills at:

Healing Jesus Campaign
Write to: evangelist@daghewardmills.org
Website: www.daghewardmills.org
Facebook: Dag Heward-Mills
Twitter: @EvangelistDag

ISBN : 978-9988-8569-0-8

Contents

CHAPTER 1

What Can Influence You?

**Another parable spake he unto them; The kingdom
of heaven is like unto leaven, which a woman took,
and hid in three measures of meal, till the whole was
leavened.**

Matthew 13:33

Leaven is an unseen, hidden influence that excites the dough and causes it to expand, rise and become lighter. Jesus Christ taught us that the kingdom of Heaven is also subject to hidden influences that affect everything.

The influence of the leaven on the dough is both real and amazing. Yet leaven is invisible when it is working mightily. Unseen influences are real. Unseen influences are good or evil.

The greatest good, unseen influence in a Christian's life is the Holy Spirit and this book is about that unseen but real influence! The sweet influences of the Holy Spirit!

This book is simply a listing of the different areas in which we can expect the influence of the Holy Spirit. We must look out for it and we must pray for it. The influence of the Holy Spirit is vital. It is most important for our survival.

What is influencing you? As a minister, what is influencing you? What is guiding you and making you do the things that you do? Are you under a good influence or under an evil influence?

There are three unseen evil influences that are largely unknown and misunderstood by Christians. The first unseen evil influence on Christians is devils. The second unseen influence on Christians is the world or the earth. The third unseen influence is our senses. When people are not under the influence of the Holy Spirit they are under one of these three influences. Thus, they are either earthly, sensual or devilish.

When writing to the Galatians, the apostle Paul warned them about invisible and pervasive influences that were affecting the church. He called these influences leavens. Paul explained the effect of a leaven. He said a leaven was a kind of persuasion. This invisible influence was so powerful that it could hinder a Christian in his ministry. Notice the Scripture: "Ye did run well; who did hinder you that ye should not obey the truth? This persuasion cometh not of him that calleth you. A little leaven leaveneth the whole lump." (Galatians 5:7-9).

This book is about the sweet influences of the Holy Spirit! It will reveal to you the different areas of your life which can be affected by the Holy Spirit. As God speaks to you through this book you will open yourself to the Holy Spirit. You will both expect and allow the Holy Spirit to influence the different aspects of your life.

CHAPTER 2

Three Evil Influences

This wisdom descendeth not from above, but is earthly, sensual, devilish.

James 3:15

The ultimate effect of the sweet influence of the Holy Spirit is to make you a spiritual person. The New Testament speaks highly of spiritual people. Spiritual people are the most important people in a church. But every human being has four options to choose from. He will either be earthly, sensual, devilish or spiritual.

Businessmen are important in the business world. Doctors are important in the health world but in the church, spiritual men are the important ones. Apostle Paul subjected his writings to spiritual men because he knew that it was only spiritual people who would know whether what he was saying was from God or not. "If any man think himself to be a prophet, or SPIRITUAL, let him acknowledge that the things that I write unto you are the commandments of the Lord" (1 Corinthians 14: 37).

You must aim to be a spiritual person who lives under the influence of the Holy Spirit. The sweet influences of the Holy Spirit will turn you into a spiritual person. On the other hand, if you do not live under the influence of the Holy Spirit you will definitely come under some other influence.

Earthly, Sensual or Devilish!

You will either be under an earthly influence, a sensual influence or a devilish influence. It is not difficult to pick out an earthly man, a sensual man or a devilish person. We see them around all the time. Instead of being spiritual, many Christians are earthly, sensual or devilish!

What is a Sensual Person Like?

A sensual person is ruled by his senses and feelings. He follows his appetites and pursues any thing he sees or likes. A sensual person will eat a lot, sleep a lot, have lots of sex and engage in any kind of pleasure that is available. Many young people start their lives by following their senses. The discos, the nightclubs and the parties are filled with people dancing away their lives and following their sensuality to its ultimate conclusion. Drug dealers and drug users are men who follow their senses to their own destruction.

A sensual person struggles to know God because it not easy to know somebody whom you cannot see.

A sensual person struggles to know God because it is not easy to know someone who is not physical. God is a spirit.

A sensual person struggles to know God because it is not easy to know someone who does not answer questions or speak.

A sensual person struggles to know God because it is not easy to know someone through a representative.

A sensual person struggles to know God because it is not easy to imagine how someone is, when he is very different from you.

A sensual person struggles to know God because it is not easy to know someone you cannot feel.

A sensual person struggles to know God because it is not easy to know someone whose voice you cannot hear.

A sensual person struggles to know God because it is not easy to know someone you have never met.

A sensual person struggles to know God because it is not easy to know someone who is mysterious.

What is an Earthly Person Like?

An earthly person has his sights set on this earth. Many sensual people metamorphose into what they think is a better version of a human being. These sensually minded people simply get converted into earthly-minded people. An earthly person has no thoughts of either Heaven or Hell. He sees no life beyond this earthly life. All his plans and pursuits reveal short-sightedness and blindness towards eternal things. Such people have no thoughts of judgement; that their acts and deeds will be brought to light and that they will pay the price for their sins.

Many decent-looking presidents and prime ministers who went to Oxford, Cambridge, Harvard, etc., once lived wild lives as young people, taking drugs, drinking and smoking endlessly. They simply changed from being sensual people and became earthly men. They may look dignified and distant from their days of sensuality. But, I tell you, many of them are simply more earthly than sensual; with no eternal values.

As a Christian your aim must be to become a spiritual man. You must not be earthly, sensual or devilish.

What is a Devilish Person Like?

A devilish person is someone who is influenced strongly by evil spirits. All unbelievers are influenced by evil spirits. However, some unbelievers speak and act under a greater influence of demon spirits.

Many people graduate from being sensual and earthly and begin to look for other meanings to life. Unfortunately they begin to find the wrong spirits.

Christians who are not spiritual can open themselves to demonic influences. Every time you open yourself to earthly and sensual sins you can be exposed to demon spirits.

What is a Spiritual Person Like?

A spiritual person has broken out of sensual influences, earthly influences and demonic influences. For sure, a spiritual person is not earthly, not sensual and not devilish.

A spiritual person bears the fruits of the spirit that are the evidence of the long-term influences of the Holy Spirit.

A spiritual person is someone who has lived under the influence of the Holy Spirit. After being under the influence of the Holy Spirit for a long time you become spiritual.

A spiritual person is therefore a mature Christian.

A spiritual person can be spoken to in a particular way. Paul said, "And I, brethren, could not speak unto you as unto spiritual, but as unto carnal, even as unto babes in Christ.

I have fed you with milk, and not with meat: for hitherto ye were not able to bear it, neither yet now are ye able.

For ye are yet carnal: for whereas there is among you envying, and strife, and divisions, are ye not carnal, and walk as men?" (1 Corinthians 3:1-3).

Indeed, the fruits of the spirit are the fruits of spirituality. They are the fruits of the long-term influence of the Holy Spirit. Love, joy, peace, patience, gentleness, meekness, humility are all evidence of spirituality. Divisions and carnality are evidence of sensuality, earthliness and demonic influences.

CHAPTER 3

The Sweet Influences of the Holy Spirit on Your Knowledge of God

We know very little about God. God cannot be seen but the evidence that He exists is all around us. Your knowledge of God is deepened in a very real way by the presence and power of the Holy Spirit. The Holy Spirit is the key to your knowledge of God.

Your knowledge of Physics, Chemistry or Biology does not depend on the Holy Spirit. Your knowledge of Chemistry depends on you being able to grasp truths that are taught and explained to you. The more logical you are, the more you may understand Mathematics, History or Psychology. But you cannot know God through processes of logic or reasoning. You will know God through the help of the Holy Spirit. You cannot know anything about God unless He helps you. That is why you must pray for the Holy Spirit's influence every time you read the Bible or listen to a message. Without the influence of the Holy Spirit you will not understand most of the things in the Bible.

Do you remember when Jesus asked Peter, *"Who do men say that I am?"* He then asked Peter, "Who do you say that I am?" When Peter said that Jesus was the Christ, Jesus recognized that the invisible Spirit of God had revealed something special to Peter. He went on to develop a closer relationship with Peter because He recognized that God had been at work in Peter, giving him the kind of knowledge and understanding he had.

You see, a child may see miracles, healings, raising of the dead, casting out of devils, powerful preaching and teaching but still not get to know God. Have you not noticed how some pastors' children sit under the teaching of the Word of God for years but grow up disbelieving the Word of God? I know children of great pastors who have declared themselves to be atheists. It is not the constant teaching and preaching of truth that converts a person. It is the powerful influence of the Holy Spirit that softens the heart of a child and turns him towards God. This is why we pray for the Holy Spirit to *move*, to *influence* and to *affect* our children. It is the Holy Spirit who softens the heart and makes them believe in God and like God.

Your personal knowledge of God and the level of revelation you have about the ministry depends entirely on what the Holy Spirit helps you to know. Without the influence of the Holy Spirit you will know very little about God and understand very little about God. That is why Jesus reacted to Peter's declaration and said, "Flesh and blood has not revealed this to you." In other words, a human being or human effort would never make you know or understand such a great and spiritual revelation.

All through the Bible, the Scripture is clear that it is the Holy Spirit who causes us to know God, to understand the Word of God and to know the truth.

How the Holy Spirit Influences Your Knowledge of God

1. *Holy Spirit Guidance into truth:* **Under the sweet influences of the Holy Spirit, you are led to truths and realities when you read the Bible.**

Howbeit when he, the Spirit of truth, is come, he will GUIDE YOU INTO ALL TRUTH: for he shall not speak of himself; but whatsoever he shall hear, that shall he speak: and he will shew you things to come.

John 16:13

2. *Holy Spirit reminders:* **When you are under the sweet influences of the Holy Spirit you are constantly reminded about the things Jesus said.**

But the Comforter, which is the Holy Ghost, whom the Father will send in my name, he shall teach you all things, and BRING ALL THINGS TO YOUR REMEMBRANCE, whatsoever I have said unto you.

John 14:26

3. *Holy Spirit direct teachings:* **When you are under the sweet influences of the Holy Spirit you are taught many things directly by God.**

But the anointing which ye have received of him abideth in you, and ye need not that any man teach you: but as THE SAME ANOINTING TEACHETH you of all things, and is truth, and is no lie, and even as it hath taught you, ye shall abide in him.

1 John 2:27

4. *Holy Spirit 'knowings':* **When you are under the sweet influences of the Holy Spirit you have "a knowing" about many things.**

But ye have an unction from the Holy One, and ye know all things.

1 John 2:20

He made known His ways to Moses, His acts to the sons of Israel.

Psalms 103:7, NASB.

5. *Holy Spirit-led ministers of God:* **When you are under the sweet influences of the anointing, you accept anointed messengers, apostles, prophets and teachers whom God has sent to you.**

And he gave some, apostles; and some, prophets; and some, evangelists; and some, pastors and teachers; for the perfecting of the saints, for the work of the ministry, for the edifying of the body of Christ:

Ephesians 4:11-12

6. *Holy Spirit communion:* **When you are under the sweet influences of the anointing, you are in constant communion with the Holy Spirit as He teaches and influences you to know God.**

The grace of the Lord Jesus Christ, and the love of God, and THE COMMUNION OF THE HOLY GHOST, be with you all. Amen.

2 Corinthians 13:14

CHAPTER 4

The Sweet Influences of the Holy Spirit on Your Prayer Life

Why You Need the Sweet Influences of the Holy Spirit to Help You Pray

1. You need the influence of the Holy Spirit to pray because it is not easy to talk to somebody you cannot see.

2. You need the influence of the Holy Spirit to pray because it is not easy to talk to somebody who does not say anything back.

3. You need the influence of the Holy Spirit to pray because you do not know what to pray for.

   Likewise the Spirit also helpeth our infirmities: for we know not what we should pray for as we ought: but the Spirit itself maketh intercession for us with groanings which cannot be uttered.
   Romans 8:26

4. You need the influence of the Holy Spirit to pray because you are spiritually discharged as you go about your daily life. Under the influence of the Holy Spirit you are charged up like a battery.

He that speaketh in an *unknown* tongue edifieth himself; but he that prophesieth edifieth the church.

1 Corinthians 14:4

5. You need the influence of the Holy Spirit to pray because otherwise most of your prayers will be directed by the flesh and by foolishness. You need the influence of the Holy Spirit to pray otherwise your prayers will be well-rehearsed phrases. When you are anointed to pray, your prayer is dictated and directed by the Holy Spirit (Acts 2:4).

6. You need the influence of the Holy Spirit to pray because without the anointing to pray, everything you say is listened to by the devil. But when you pray in tongues devils do not understand what you are saying.

Follow after charity, and desire spiritual gifts, but rather that ye may prophesy.

1 Corinthians 14:1

7. You need the influence of the Holy Spirit to pray because through that influence you will know the mind of the Spirit. When you pray in tongues you can hear the voice of the Spirit by interpreting your prayer.

Wherefore let him that speaketh in an unknown tongue pray that he may interpret.

1 Corinthians 14:13

8. You need the influence of the Holy Spirit to pray because it is difficult to pray for a long time. When you are under the influence of the Holy Spirit you will be able to pray for long hours like Jesus.

And in the morning, rising up a great while before day, he went out, and departed into a solitary place, and there prayed.

Mark 1:35

And it came to pass in those days, that he went out into a mountain to pray, and continued all night in prayer to God.

Luke 6:12

9. You need the influence of the Holy Spirit to pray because your mind wanders when you pray. Under the influence of the Holy Spirit you can speak in tongues and to God. This helps you to concentrate on God everywhere you are.

    But if there be no interpreter, let him keep silence in the church; and LET HIM SPEAK TO HIMSELF, AND TO GOD.

    1 Corinthians 14:28

10. You need the influence of the Holy Spirit to pray because in the natural you may not have a grateful attitude. But when you are anointed to pray you can give thanks well.

    For thou verily givest thanks well, but the other is not edified.

    1 Corinthians 14:17

How the Holy Spirit Influenced the Prayer Lives of Christians

1. **The Holy Spirit helped the infirmities of the believers by helping them to pray.**

    Likewise the Spirit also helpeth our infirmities: for we know not what we should pray for as we ought: but the Spirit itself maketh intercession for us with groanings which cannot be uttered.

    Romans 8:26

2. **When the disciples in the upper room came under the influence of the Holy Spirit they began to pray in tongues on the day of Pentecost.**

    And when the day of Pentecost was fully come, they were all with one accord in one place.

And suddenly there came a sound from heaven as of a rushing mighty wind, and it filled all the house where they were sitting.

And there appeared unto them cloven tongues like as of fire, and it sat upon each of them.

And THEY WERE ALL FILLED WITH THE HOLY GHOST, AND BEGAN TO SPEAK WITH OTHER TONGUES, AS THE SPIRIT GAVE THEM UTTERANCE.

Acts 2:1-4

3. **When the household of Cornelius came under the sweet influence of the Holy Spirit they began to pray in tongues.**

While Peter yet spake these words, THE HOLY GHOST FELL ON ALL THEM which heard the word.

And they of the circumcision which believed were astonished, as many as came with Peter, because that on the Gentiles also was poured out the gift of the Holy Ghost.

For THEY HEARD THEM SPEAK WITH TONGUES, and magnify God. Then answered Peter,Can any man forbid water, that these should not be baptized, which have received the Holy Ghost as well as we?

Acts 10:44-47

4. **When the disciples in Ephesus came under the sweet influence of the Holy Spirit they began to pray in tongues.**

And it came to pass, that, while Apollos was at Corinth, Paul having passed through the upper coasts came to Ephesus: and finding certain disciples,

And when Paul had laid his hands upon them, the Holy Ghost came on them; and they spake with tongues, and prophesied.

And all the men were about twelve.

Acts 19:1, 6-7

If you are not under the sweet influence of the Holy Spirit, you will be under earthly, sensual or devilish influences that will lead you not to pray.

When you are not under the influence of the Holy Spirit, you will not believe in the importance of prayer. You will become prayerless and powerless. You will believe that you can solve problems by using your natural strength instead of reaching out to God in prayer.

Your life will be governed by the senses and not by God. This is because a sensual person lives his life serving the lusts of his flesh and his mind. You will be too lazy to pray! You will need food, rest and pleasure all the time and therefore have no time to pray.

If you are not under the sweet influence of the Holy Spirit you will be subject to devilish influences which will make you seek power elsewhere. Witchcraft, occult and other demonic sources will become the source of your power.

When you come under a devilish influence you will be opposed to prayer and deny its power. This is because a devilish influence will lead you away from a relationship with God through prayer.

The sweet influence of the Holy Spirit is the anointing for prayer. It is the supernatural ability and grace given to a believer to pray.

The sweet influence of the anointing gives you the ability to speak in tongues because every time the anointing for prayer fell on people they began to speak in tongues. The anointing for prayer was given several times in the book of Acts.

How to Yield to the Sweet Influences of the Holy Spirit to Pray

1. **Open yourself to the sweet influences of the Holy Spirit by praying in tongues and thinking about what you need to think about.**

For if I pray in an *unknown* tongue, my spirit prayeth, but my understanding is unfruitful.

1 Corinthians 14:14

2. Open yourself to the sweet influences of the Holy Spirit by praying in tongues and studying.

For if I pray in an *unknown* tongue, my spirit prayeth, but my understanding is unfruitful.

1 Corinthians 14:14

3. Open yourself to the sweet influences of the Holy Spirit by praying in tongues and reading the Bible.

For if I pray in an *unknown* tongue, my spirit prayeth, but my understanding is unfruitful.

1 Corinthians 14:14

4. Open yourself to the sweet influence of the Holy Spirit by praying in tongues and reading other books.

For if I pray in an *unknown* tongue, my spirit prayeth, but my understanding is unfruitful.

1 Corinthians 14:14

5. Open yourself to the sweet influences of the Holy Spirit by praying in tongues and listening to CDs.

For if I pray in an *unknown* tongue, my spirit prayeth, but my understanding is unfruitful.

1 Corinthians 14:14

6. Open yourself to the sweet influence of the Holy Spirit by praying in tongues and watching videos.

For if I pray in an *unknown* tongue, my spirit prayeth, but my understanding is unfruitful.

1 Corinthians 14:14

7. **Open yourself to the sweet influences of the Holy Spirit by praying in tongues and dressing up.**

For if I pray in an *unknown* tongue, my spirit prayeth, but my understanding is unfruitful.

1 Corinthians 14:14

8. **Open yourself to the sweet influences of the Holy Spirit by praying in tongues and walking.**

For if I pray in an unknown tongue, my spirit prayeth, but my understanding is unfruitful.

1 Corinthians 14:14

9. **Open yourself to the sweet influences of the Holy Spirit by praying in tongues and working in the office.**

For if I pray in an unknown tongue, my spirit prayeth, but my understanding is unfruitful.

1 Corinthians 14:14

10. **Open yourself to the sweet influences of the Holy Spirit by praying in tongues and driving your car.**

For if I pray in an unknown tongue, my spirit prayeth, but my understanding is unfruitful.

1 Corinthians 14:14

CHAPTER 5

The Sweet Influences of the Anointing on Your Ability to Be Holy

Without the help of the Holy Spirit you will live out your life like every other person without boundaries and limits. You will yield yourself to the flesh and fulfil the lusts of your mind. Human beings who are not supernaturally restrained by the Holy Spirit are lazy, wicked, thieves, fornicators, witches, drunkards, murderers and rapists.

It takes great supernatural power to turn away from the course of this world. In our world today, it is unusual to be chaste or holy. It is normal to be a person with multiple sexual partners. You cannot blame people who have no supernatural power helping them. Most of the sins of the flesh are outbursts of naturalness and humanness. These outbursts of human behaviour have created the evil world in which we live. Through the depravities, selfishness and greed of mankind, a hard and wicked society called the world has been created. Paul said, we once walked according to the course of this world and fulfilled the desires of our flesh and mind, just like everybody else.

And you were dead in your trespasses and sins, in which you formerly walked according to the course of this world, ACCORDING TO THE PRINCE of the power of the air, of the spirit that is now working in the sons of disobedience.
Among them we too all formerly lived in the lusts of our flesh, INDULGING THE DESIRES OF THE FLESH AND OF THE MIND, and were by nature children of wrath, even as the rest.

Ephesians 2:2-3 (NASB)

When you are not under the sweet influences of the Holy Spirit you will be subject to devilish influences, which will make you practice all the sins of the flesh. That is why you must open yourself up to be influenced by the Holy Spirit. The Holy Spirit's influence will cause you to be holy, special and different.

I am not trying to give you steps on how to be holy. I am informing you about what happens to you when you are under the influence of the Holy Spirit. Are you holy? Are you pure? Are you clean? Are you straight? (Do you have skeletons in your cupboard?) Are you real? Are you sanctified? If you are any of these things then it is by the power and influence of the Holy Spirit. Pray for the Holy Spirit. Ask God for the Holy Spirit to come and help you to be holy, sanctified and pure. You can never be pure with your own strength. You cannot be a virgin unless the Holy Spirit helps you.

Do you want to stop living the life of fleshly fulfilment? You need the Holy Spirit to help you become pure. Pray for the Holy Spirit! Ask for the Holy Spirit! He will help you! You cannot make it on your own. You will never be successful at being holy, no matter how long you have been a Christian. If the Holy Spirit leaves you for one day you will become a normal man to your own surprise. Don't trust in yourself or you will disgrace yourself. The Scripture confirms these amazing truths.

How the Holy Spirit Influences
Your Ability to Be Holy

1. **The Holy Spirit enables you to resist the lusts of your flesh.** The sweet influence of the Holy Spirit puts you under a supernatural power that enables you to not fulfil, obey or yield to the desires of your flesh. Without the influence of the Holy Spirit, you will be consumed by the raging desires that are common to all men.

    This I say then, WALK IN THE SPIRIT, AND YE SHALL NOT FULFIL THE LUST of the flesh. For the flesh lusteth against the Spirit, and the Spirit against the flesh: and these are contrary the one to the other: so that ye cannot do the things that ye would.

    Galatians 5:16-17

2. **The Holy Spirit has a sanctifying influence.** The influence of the Holy Spirit tends towards sanctification, purity and holiness. Expect to live a life of greater purity, sanctification and holiness when under the sweet influence of the Holy Spirit.

    According to the foreknowledge of God the Father, by the SANCTIFYING WORK OF THE SPIRIT, that you may obey Jesus Christ and be sprinkled with His blood: May grace and peace be yours in the fullest measure.

    1 Peter 1:2 (NASB)

CHAPTER 6

The Sweet Influences of the Holy Spirit on Your Spiritual Strength

Why You Need the Sweet Influences of the Holy Spirit to Give You Spiritual Strength

You need supernatural strength because of your weak frame. "Like as a father pitieth his children, so the Lord pitieth them that fear him. For HE KNOWETH OUR FRAME; he remembereth that we are dust" (Psalms 103:13-14). The weakness of your frame causes you to drop behind and fail all the time. You are unable to make the mark because your frame is weak. The only hope that you have is the Holy Spirit who will strengthen you with power in the inner man.

You need supernatural strength to overcome all your enemies. Spiritual strength is the supernatural ability a believer has to overcome the temptations in this world. Without the influence of the Holy Spirit that makes you spiritually strong, you will not be able to overcome most temptations.

You need strength to overcome the challenges every Christian experiences.

Through the inner workings of the Holy Spirit you will become a strong minister of the gospel. You will survive withering storms through the influence of the Holy Spirit. You will be standing when others have fallen. You will be upright when others are bent over.

How the Holy Spirit Gives Strength

1. **The sweet influence of the Holy Spirit gives strength by imparting "might" to you in the inner man.** How exactly does the Holy Spirit minister this "might" to a man? I don't know! But I do know that it is real. There is something called "might." This "might" is imparted into your spirit and then you become stronger and stronger in the Lord. Pray for the Holy Spirit to make you strong.

   For this cause I bow my knees unto the Father of our Lord Jesus Christ,

   Of whom the whole family in heaven and earth is named,

   That he would grant you, according to the riches of his glory, to be STRENGTHENED WITH MIGHT BY HIS SPIRIT in the inner man;

   Ephesians 3:14-16

2. **The sweet influence of the Holy Spirit gives strength when the spirit of "might" rests upon you.** This is a prophecy which reveals the source of the strength of Jesus Christ. Jesus was spiritually strong. He overcame all temptations that He encountered. He destroyed the works of the devil and ministered the power of God with great strength. But how did He become so strong? The spirit of "might" rested upon Him!

   And the spirit of the Lord shall rest upon him, the spirit of wisdom and understanding, THE SPIRIT OF counsel and MIGHT, the spirit of knowledge and of the fear of the LORD;

   Isaiah 11:2

CHAPTER 7

The Sweet Influences of the Holy Spirit on Your Physical Strength

Strength comes from body-building. Strength comes from eating well and exercising properly. Indeed, this is true but a Christian must know and believe that there is also strength that comes from the spirit realm. An evil spirit can give a man supernatural strength over and beyond what comes from body-building or weight lifting.

The Holy Spirit can also give a person supernatural physical strength. The Bible is full of examples of human beings receiving supernatural strength from the spirit realm. When you are under the influence of the Holy Spirit, you receive strength from the Lord. This is why you do not feel tired, weak or sick when you are ministering under the anointing. Many people experience the symptoms of their sickness when they finish ministering and come off the platform. Sometimes, when you are ministering under the anointing of the Holy Spirit, all symptoms of sickness will disappear.

You may still be on the platform when the anointing of the Holy Spirit begins to lift off you. The sign of the departure of the Holy Spirit upon you will often be the return of the symptoms of weakness or sickness which you felt before the anointing was on you to minister.

Sometimes, the anointing will lift and sometimes return to you. Each time the anointing lifts, you may feel certain symptoms or weakness but when the anointing returns, these symptoms will simply vanish. Indeed, both physical and spiritual strength are impartations that come through the influence of the Holy Spirit.

How exactly do you become physically strong when the Holy Spirit comes upon you? The answer is, I do not know! But I do not need to know how it happens. All I need to know is that the presence of the Holy Spirit affects my level of physical strength. Once I am aware of this reality, I become sensitive to the workings of the Holy Spirit.

Six Examples of Physical Strength that Came from the Spirit Realm

1. An evil spirit gave one man enough strength to overcome seven sons of Sceva.

And there were SEVEN SONS of one Sceva, a Jew, and chief of the priests, which did so.

And THE EVIL SPIRIT answered and said, Jesus I know, and Paul I know; but who are ye?

And the man in whom THE EVIL SPIRIT was leaped on them, and OVERCAME THEM, and prevailed against them, so that THEY FLED out of that house naked and wounded.

Acts 19:14-16

2. An unclean spirit gave the mad man of Gadara so much strength that no one could chain him.

And when he was come out of the ship, immediately there met him out of the tombs A MAN WITH AN UNCLEAN SPIRIT,

Who had his dwelling among the tombs; and NO MAN COULD BIND HIM, no, not with chains:

Because that he had been often bound with fetters and chains, and the chains had been plucked asunder by him, and the fetters broken in pieces: neither could any man tame him.

Mark 5:2-4

3. The Holy Spirit gave Samson so much supernatural strength that he killed a lion as though he was killing a goat.

Then went Samson down, and his father and his mother, to Timnath, and came to the vineyards of Timnath: and, behold, a young LION roared against him.

And the SPIRIT OF THE LORD CAME MIGHTILY UPON HIM, AND HE RENT HIM AS HE WOULD HAVE RENT A KID, and he had nothing in his hand: but he told not his father or his mother what he had done.

Judges 14:5-6

4. The Holy Spirit gave Samson supernatural strength to kill thirty men all by himself.

Then THE SPIRIT OF THE LORD CAME UPON HIM mightily, and he went down to Ashkelon and KILLED THIRTY OF THEM and took their spoil, and gave the changes of clothes to those who told the riddle. And his anger burned, and he went up to his father's house.

Judges 14:19 (NASB)

5. The Holy Spirit gave Samson supernatural strength to kill a thousand men with a jawbone.

And when he came unto Lehi, the Philistines shouted against him: and THE SPIRIT OF THE LORD CAME MIGHTILY UPON HIM, and the cords that were upon his arms became as flax that was burnt with fire, and his bands loosed from off his hands.

And he found a new jawbone of an ass, and put forth his hand, and took it, and SLEW A THOUSAND MEN THEREWITH.

Judges 15:14-15

6. The Holy Spirit gave Jesus supernatural strength to overcome in the wilderness.

And Jesus being full of the Holy Ghost returned from Jordan, and was led by the Spirit into the wilderness, Being forty days tempted of the devil.

Luke 4:1-2

CHAPTER 8

The Sweet Influences of the Anointing on Your Level of Intelligence

The Four Pillars of Intelligence

Intelligence is defined as the capacity for learning, reasoning and understanding. It is the aptitude for grasping truths, relationships, facts and meanings.

The four pillars of intelligence are knowledge, wisdom, understanding and the fear of the Lord. The Holy Spirit influences your knowledge, your wisdom, your understanding and your fear of the Lord. All these four aspects make up intelligence.

Amazingly, the Holy Spirit influences each of these areas directly.

Knowledge is the information that you need. It consists of the facts, the data and the truths about any subject. Thankfully, the Holy Spirit is a source of knowledge. A great part of His influence is to cause you to have knowledge. Ignorance is directly proportional to many of the evils in the world today. The more people are uneducated and ignorant, the higher the levels of poverty, disease, backwardness, wars and famine.

The Holy Spirit's Influence on Your Level of Knowledge

1. **Your level of knowledge is directly influenced by the Holy Spirit because the Holy Spirit is the spirit of knowledge.**

And the spirit of the LORD shall rest upon him, the spirit of wisdom and understanding, the spirit of counsel and might, the spirit of knowledge and of the fear of the LORD;

Isaiah 11:2

The Holy Spirit's Influence on Your Level of Wisdom

Your level of wisdom is directly influenced by the Holy Spirit because the Holy Spirit is the spirit of wisdom. Wisdom is the ability to apply the knowledge that you have. Wisdom is the ability to apply the experience that you have. Wisdom is the ability to apply the common sense that you have. Wisdom is the ability to apply the insight that you have. Wisdom is the ability to apply the understanding that you have.

Many presidents of many countries are highly educated. They know a lot of things that they learnt on the way to becoming presidents. Many of them acquired knowledge in schools like Oxford, Cambridge, Harvard and the like. However, many lack the ability to apply their knowledge, common sense and information in their countries. The quality that enables a person to use the knowledge he has acquired is called wisdom. Sometimes, it is as though the knowledge these people learn evaporates when they land at the airport of their home countries.

Fortunately, the Holy Spirit is also a source of wisdom. In fact, He is called the spirit of wisdom.

That the God of our Lord Jesus Christ, the Father of glory, may give unto you the spirit of wisdom and revelation in the knowledge of him:

Ephesians 1:17

The Holy Spirit's Influence on Your Level of Understanding

Understanding is the ability to grasp truths. It is the ability to comprehend and interpret what is being said. When someone lacks the ability to comprehend or interpret the meaning of what you said, we describe the person as lacking understanding. Understanding is also the inclination of a person to agree or to flow with an opinion. A man of understanding has the capacity for rational thinking and reasoning.

Thankfully, the Holy Spirit is also the spirit of understanding. Through the influence of the Holy Spirit, your ability to interpret statements and reason with others will be greater. Through the Holy Spirit, your capacity to think rationally will increase and improve.

A man of understanding is greatly promoted in this life and becomes far greater than a man without understanding. "Get wisdom, get understanding: forget it not; neither decline from the words of my mouth. Forsake her not, and she shall preserve thee: love her, and she shall keep thee.

Wisdom is the principal thing; therefore get wisdom: and with all thy getting get understanding.

Exalt her, and she shall promote thee: she shall bring thee to honour, when thou dost embrace her. She shall give to thine head an ornament of grace: a crown of glory shall she deliver to thee" (Proverbs 4:5-9).

Your level of understanding is directly influenced by the Holy Spirit because the Holy Spirit is the spirit of understanding.

The eyes of your understanding being enlightened; that ye may know what is the hope of his calling, and what the riches of the glory of his inheritance in the saints,

Ephesians 1:18

31

The Holy Spirit's Influence on Your Fear of the Lord

The extent to which you fear God is directly influenced by the Holy Spirit because the Holy Spirit is the spirit of the fear of the Lord. The fear of the Lord is the respect for the God-factor. That there is a God who rules in the affairs of men is a truth that will be strong on the hearts of anyone who fears God. Without the fear of God, all knowledge, all wisdom and all understanding amount to nothing. You are reduced to the level of an animal because you did not retain God in your knowledge. "And even as they did not like to retain God in their knowledge, God gave them over to a reprobate mind, to do those things which are not convenient" (Romans 1:28).

If you invented the rocket, the computer, the mobile phone, the aeroplane and the helicopter and you do not believe in God, you are not wise but a fool. Your knowledge, your wisdom and your understanding of these wonderful inventions will amount to nothing and you will be judged a fool.

And the spirit of the LORD shall rest upon him, the spirit of wisdom and understanding, the spirit of counsel and might, the spirit of knowledge and of THE FEAR OF THE LORD;

And shall make him of quick understanding in THE FEAR OF THE LORD: and he shall not judge after the sight of his eyes, neither reprove after the hearing of his ears:

Isaiah 11:2-3

How to Know When the Influence of the Anointing Is Ministering Wisdom into Your Life

You will discern the influence of the Holy Spirit when you sense a certain kind of wisdom. The kind of wisdom that comes from the influence of the Holy Spirit is pure, peaceful, gentle, easy to be entreated, full of mercy and good fruits, full of mercy, without partiality and without hypocrisy.

The Holy Spirit will teach you that it is wise to be pure. The Holy Spirit will teach you that it is wise to be peaceful. The Holy Spirit will teach you that it is wise to be gentle. The Holy Spirit will teach you that it is wise to be easy to be entreated. The Holy Spirit will teach you that it is wise to be full of good fruits and mercy. The Holy Spirit will teach you that it is wise to be without partiality. The Holy Spirit will teach you that it is wise to be without hypocrisy.

As you sense this kind of counsel in life, you will be recognizing the influence of the anointing and the Holy Spirit.

How to Know When the Influence of the Anointing Is Ministering Knowledge into Your Life

You will know that the influence of the Holy Spirit is giving you knowledge when the knowledge that is coming to you has certain characteristics. The kind of knowledge that comes from the influence of the Holy Spirit has certain characteristics. The knowledge that comes from God ministers grace and peace. The knowledge that comes from God is useful for all aspects of your life and your godliness. There are lots of subjects that we learn in school that have no usefulness to our lives. There are lots of things we know that do not help us to be godly. As the Holy Spirit ministers knowledge to you your intelligence will increase and you will know many things that are very useful for your life.

Grace and peace be multiplied unto you THROUGH THE KNOWLEDGE of God, and of Jesus our Lord,

According as his divine power hath given unto us all things that pertain unto life and godliness, THROUGH THE KNOWLEDGE of him that hath called us to glory and virtue:

2 Peter 1:2-3

How to Know When the Influence of the Anointing Is Ministering Understanding into Your Life

You will know that the influence of the Holy Spirit is bringing understanding to your life when you are more inclined to flow with the knowledge of God and with the mysteries of God.

When you have more understanding, the mysteries of God are within your reach. You are able to attain to wise counsel.

A wise man will hear, and will increase learning; and a man of understanding shall attain unto wise counsels:

Proverbs 1:5

People without understanding are not able to attain to wisdom. They cannot understand the preacher's "Seven Steps". They cannot read the books because they cannot understand them. They cannot understand the simplest precepts and the simplest ideas that the preacher is constantly sharing. People without understanding are left out of certain meetings. People without understanding drag meetings and belabour certain points that everyone else understands.

You must be careful when you are dealing with a person without understanding. He may even think you are insulting or cursing him when you make a simple point at a meeting. People without understanding feel easily insulted and looked down upon. A man of understanding must understand when he is dealing with a man without understanding.

How to Know When the Influence of the Anointing Is Ministering the Fear of the Lord into Your Life

The fear of the Lord is the spirit of the fear of the Lord. The more you respect God and fear His role in whatever you do, the more you have the influence of the Holy Spirit in you. As you come under the influence of the Holy Spirit, you will fear God more and more and you will be afraid and terrified that he may strike you down at any moment for anything.

You will recognize more and more his divine hand in the affairs of men and you will set aside the notion that things work out by chance. As the Holy Spirit influences you concerning the fear of God you will become sure that principles are real, but God overrules all principles to ensure His will is done. You will know that God rules.

CHAPTER 9

The Sweet Influences of the Holy Spirit on Your Character

But the FRUIT OF THE SPIRIT is love, joy, peace, longsuffering, gentleness, goodness, faith, Meekness, temperance: against such there is no law.

Galatians 5:22-23

Under the sweet influence of the Holy Spirit, you have the supernatural ability and grace to bear the fruits of the Spirit. Without the influence of the Holy Spirit you will be an ordinary man; full of greed, selfishness, lust, impatience, discontentment, suspicion, mistrust and evil thoughts and pride.

When you come under the influence of the Holy Spirit, you develop a completely different set of character traits. You virtually change into a different person.

Instead of lust you are full of love.

Instead of discontentment you are full of joy and peace.

Instead of impatience you are full of longsuffering and gentleness.

Instead of wickedness you are full of goodness.

Instead of mistrust and suspicion you are full of faith.

Instead of pride and arrogance you are full of meekness and temperance.

Naturally human beings are not full of love and joy, peace, longsuffering, gentleness, goodness, faith, meekness and temperance.

Allow the Holy Spirit to influence you and bring out these wonderful character traits. Embrace every experience in life as a God-given opportunity to bear fruit.

Why do you think no one wants to marry you? Why do you think no one wants to be with you? Why do you think you cannot keep a team together? Love never fails.

You must allow the Holy Spirit to change your character and make you enjoyable to be with. Are you quarrelsome or are you peaceful? Are you irksome or are you full of temperance?

Are you full of lust or you are full of love? Are you under the influence of the Holy Spirit or you are under a sensual and devilish influence?

When the sweet influence of the Holy Spirit is strong in your life you will be able to wait for God's timing in everything.

You can always tell when someone has been under the influence of the Holy Spirit for some time. You will see by the fruits in his life and her life. She may be pretty on the outside, having earthly influences that give her good hairstyles, good necklaces and nice make-up. But it takes the influence of the Holy Spirit to have a nice character.

Are you impressed with the make-up and the nice dresses? Then the earthly and sensual influences on the lady are working on you. Are you impressed with her love, joy, peace and meekness? Then the sweet influences of the Holy Spirit on the lady are drawing you.

It is time to pray in the spirit and open yourself to that wonderful influence from above.

CHAPTER 10

The Sweet Influences of the Holy Spirit on Your Ability to Love

And hope maketh not ashamed; because THE LOVE OF GOD IS SHED abroad in our hearts BY THE HOLY GHOST which is given unto us.

Romans 5:5

The key sign of your inability to love is your broken relationships and friendships that should have been life-long relationships! Most of the relationships God gives you are to last a lifetime. Because of your inability to walk in love, many of your relationships do not last very long.

The sweet influence of the Holy Spirit imparts a supernatural ability to walk in love and to forgive. Even though you are born again, the flesh is still the same. Without the help of the Holy Spirit you will not be able to walk in love and you will not be able to genuinely forgive. There are many ministers who claim to be heavily anointed with the power of the Holy Spirit and yet cannot walk in the love of God.

Making people fall down and having mighty spiritual manifestations is not the same as walking in love. Walking and operating in love is a cardinal sign of the presence of the Spirit.

I remember a long-standing pastor who was so offended that he could not continue to be a member of the church. The effect of his hurt was almost palpable as he seethed with rage and offense. No one could speak to him, no one could counsel him and no one could make him see reason. It is such people that make me understand how someone who hates his brother is a murderer. You can virtually see murder in the eyes of some pastors.

Everyone says, "I have forgiven him and I do not have any grudge against anyone." But they do, and it shows in their lives and in their actions. You cannot make a claim to the presence of the Holy Spirit if you cannot walk in divine love and forgiveness.

This is why we need the Holy Spirit. There is a great love that comes into your life from the Holy Spirit. It is called the love of the Spirit (Romans 15:30). The Holy Spirit pours love into your heart and enables you to practice it. Pray for the Holy Spirit to come on your life. Supernaturally, you will be able to love even the most unlovable and unforgivable human being. It is called the love of the Spirit.

Now I beseech you, brethren, for the Lord Jesus Christ's sake, and for the LOVE OF THE SPIRIT, that ye strive together with me in your prayers to God for me;

Romans 15:30

When you go close to men who walk with the Holy Spirit you often find love. Often, you will not be impressed by the great truths they stand for but by the great love they seem to have. Love is best enjoyed at close range. As you get closer to men who are under a real anointing, you start to experience the great love they have for God and for men.

Pray for the Holy Spirit. Expect God to give you the power to love and to forgive. It is the key sign of the presence of the Holy Spirit's work in your life and ministry.

CHAPTER 11

The Sweet Influences of the Anointing on Your Ministry Style

And he shall go before him in THE SPIRIT AND POWER OF ELIAS, to turn the hearts of the fathers to the children, and the disobedient to the wisdom of the just; to make ready a people prepared for the Lord.

Luke 1:17

This is a prophecy given to Zechariah, the father of John the Baptist, about his son. In this prophecy, it was clear that he was to have a son who would walk under the same influence of the spirit that Elijah did. The prophecy was direct! The little boy would be influenced by the same Spirit and the same power that influenced Elijah. After John the Baptist began his ministry, many came to him and received a blessing. But it was Jesus who pointed out that John the Baptist was walking under the same influence of the Holy Spirit as Elijah. He said to His disciples, "And if ye will receive it, this is Elias, which was for to come" (Matthew 11:14).

It was clear that John the Baptist was flowing in a special anointing. That anointing of the Holy Spirit on Elijah was the same as that on John the Baptist. What did this anointing do? What did this special influence of the Holy Spirit do? It gave birth to a similar style of ministry! Amazingly, the similarities in the style of ministry are carefully described in the Scriptures.

Notice, and do not be surprised, if the Holy Spirit gives you a ministry that is similar to someone else's. Do not listen to fruitless trees that criticise you for copying. These empty clouds have achieved nothing and are constantly frightening up and coming ministers from learning all they can from mentors and fathers. Go ahead and learn all you can! If God gives you a similar style to someone you love, then accept it and flow in it! You may be surprised that you are the John the Baptist who is walking in the footsteps of an Elijah! Once something is carefully chronicled in the Bible, you must not be afraid of it. What you must be afraid of are the things that are not in the Bible. Do not be afraid of developing the style of ministry of the wonderful men whom God has raised up in front of you.

How the Holy Spirit Influenced
Elijah's Style of Ministry

1. The Holy Spirit influenced Elijah on where he lived.

So he went and did according unto the word of the LORD: for he went and dwelt by the brook Cherith, that is before Jordan.

1 Kings 17:5

2. The Holy Spirit influenced Elijah on what he ate.

And the ravens brought him bread and flesh in the morning, and bread and flesh in the evening; and he drank of the brook.

1 Kings 17:6

3. The Holy Spirit influenced Elijah on what he wore.

And they answered him, He was an hairy man, and girt with a girdle of leather about his loins. And he said, it is Elijah the Tishbite.

2 Kings 1:8

4. The Holy Spirit influenced Elijah to confront the king.

And it came to pass, when Ahab saw Elijah, that Ahab said unto him, Art thou he that troubleth Israel? And he answered, I have not troubled Israel; but thou, and thy father's house, in that ye have forsaken the commandments of the LORD, and thou hast followed Baalim.

1 Kings 18:17-18

And Ahab said to Elijah, Hast thou found me, O mine enemy? And he answered, I have found thee: because thou hast sold thyself to work evil in the sight of the LORD.

1 Kings 21:20

5. **The Holy Spirit influenced Elijah to confront powerful women.**

And of Jezebel also spake the LORD, saying, the dogs shall eat Jezebel by the wall of Jezreel.

1 Kings 21:23

How the Holy Spirit Influenced John the Baptist's Style of Ministry

1. **The Holy Spirit influenced John the Baptist on where he lived.**

The voice of one crying in the wilderness, Prepare ye the way of the Lord, make his paths straight.

John did baptize in the wilderness, and preach the baptism of repentance for the remission of sins.

Mark 1:3-4

2. **The Holy Spirit influenced John the Baptist on what he ate.**

And John ... did eat locusts and wild honey

Mark 1:6

3. **The Holy Spirit influenced John the Baptist on what he wore.**

And John was clothed with camel's hair, and with a girdle of a skin about his loins…

Mark 1:6

4. **The Holy Spirit influenced John the Baptist to confront the king.**

But Herod the tetrarch, being reproved by him for Herodias his brother Philip's wife, and for all the evils which Herod had done, Added yet this above all, that he shut up John in prison.

Luke 3:19-20

5. The Holy Spirit influenced John the Baptist to confront powerful women.

For John had said unto Herod, It is not lawful for thee to have thy brother's wife.

Therefore Herodias had a quarrel against him, and would have killed him; but she could not:

Mark 6:18-19

If you are under the sweet influence of the Spirit you will have a ministry style that is from Heaven.

Elijah was under the anointing of the Holy Spirit, and the sweet influences of the Holy Spirit changed his personality. His personality made him wear little shorts, live in the desert and eat worms. The Holy Spirit also made him have a confrontational ministry.

John the Baptist also came under the same influence of the Spirit. This influence and anointing made John the Baptist behave in the exact same way. He also lived in the desert, and wore little panties. He ate locusts and wild honey for dessert. What a shock! This similarity between John the Baptist and Elijah can be attributed to the same kind of anointing that rested on them.

The alternative to this is to have a ministry style that is earthly, sensual or devilish. Today, most of us have adopted the style of an earthly chief executive officer. Those of us who claim to be men of God resemble worldly millionaire chief executives more than we do biblical prophets. This is because the earthly influence on our lives is more than the influence of the Holy Spirit.

The composers of today's Christian music have taken on earthly, sensual and sometimes demonic styles. Sensual singers and sensual songs are released by Christian artistes. Our music and our books are so earthly that they have a crossover appeal and attract the world. Instead of being ashamed that our songs can be played in discos, we are glad that our music is popular in the world. The love of money, which is the root of all evil, is closely linked to the love of popularity and power.

Christian books and even Christian preaching have an appeal to the masses of this world and we are unable to diagnose that we are more under an earthly, sensual influence than under the sweet influences of the Holy Spirit.

Under the sweet influence of the Holy Spirit, the influence of money and popularity with its crossover appeal will die.

Much Christian preaching is not influenced by the Holy Spirit but by the influence of this earth. Large churches are filled with sensual baby Christians who love money and all the world has to offer. You are not likely to go into a church today and hear a sermon entitled, "Do not lay up riches on earth." You must rather expect to hear, "Seven keys to abundant riches."

"Heaven will take care of itself," they say. "We must have abundant life now and here."

Are we the ministers of the gospel under the influence of the Holy Spirit or are we under the influence of the world?

CHAPTER 12

The Sweet Influences of the Holy Spirit on Your Ministry Achievements

Elisha was promised a double portion of the anointing that was on Elijah. It is evident that Elisha received a double portion of the anointing of the Holy Spirit. Because the anointing of the Holy Spirit on Elisha was the same as that on Elijah they both achieved similar things in ministry. The Holy Spirit does not only affect your ministry style. He also affects the things you achieve for God. Amazingly, both Elijah and Elisha achieved similar things in the name of the Lord. The Scripture is so clear on this reality.

I firmly believe that every achievement of a man of God is because of the influence of the Holy Spirit on his life. If you want to achieve what someone has achieved you must receive the Holy Spirit to the same extent that he has and you must come under the influence of the Holy Spirit to the same extent that he has.

If you want to build a church to the same extent that certain pastors have, you must come under the influence of the Holy Spirit to the same extent and in the same way that they have. It is simple! Every achievement in ministry is the direct product of the influences of the Holy Spirit.

How the Holy Spirit Influenced Elijah's Achievements in Ministry

1. The Holy Spirit influenced Elijah to raise the dead.

And it came to pass after these things, that the son of the woman, the mistress of the house, fell sick; and his sickness was so sore, that there was no breath left in him.

And she said unto Elijah, What have I to do with thee, O thou man of God? art thou come unto me to call my sin to remembrance, and to slay my son?

And he said unto her, Give me thy son. And he took him out of her bosom, and carried him up into a loft, where he abode, and laid him upon his own bed.

And he cried unto the LORD, and said, O LORD my God, hast thou also brought evil upon the widow with whom I sojourn, by slaying her son?

And he stretched himself upon the child three times, and cried unto the LORD, and said, O LORD my God, I pray thee, let this child's soul come into him again.

And the LORD heard the voice of Elijah; and the soul of the child came into him again, and he revived.

1 Kings 17:17-22

2. The Holy Spirit influenced Elijah to prevent the rain.

And Elijah the Tishbite, who was of the inhabitants of Gilead, said unto Ahab, As the LORD God of Israel liveth, before whom I stand, there shall not be dew nor rain these years, but according to my word.

1 Kings 17:1

3. The Holy Spirit influenced Elijah to minister to widows.

And Elijah said unto her, Fear not; go and do as thou hast said: but make me thereof a little cake first, and bring it unto me, and after make for thee and for thy son.

49

For thus saith the LORD God of Israel, The barrel of meal shall not waste, neither shall the cruse of oil fail, until the day that the LORD sendeth rain upon the earth.

And she went and did according to the saying of Elijah: and she, and he, and her house, did eat many days.

And the barrel of meal wasted not, neither did the cruse of oil fail, according to the word of the LORD, which he spake by Elijah.

1 Kings 17:13-16

4. The Holy Spirit influenced Elijah to part the water.

And Elijah took his mantle, and wrapped it together, and smote the waters, and they were divided hither and thither, so that they two went over on dry ground.

2 Kings 2:8

How the Holy Spirit Influenced Elisha's Achievements in Ministry

1. The Holy Spirit influenced Elisha to raise the dead.

And when Elisha was come into the house, behold, the child was dead, and laid upon his bed.

He went in therefore, and shut the door upon them twain, and prayed unto the LORD.

And he went up, and lay upon the child, and put his mouth upon his mouth, and his eyes upon his eyes, and his hands upon his hands: and he stretched himself upon the child; and the flesh of the child waxed warm.

Then he returned, and walked in the house to and fro; and went up, and stretched himself upon him: and the child sneezed seven times, and the child opened his eyes.

2 Kings 4:32-35

2. The Holy Spirit influenced Elisha to prevent the rain.

For thus saith the Lord, Ye shall not see wind, neither shall ye see rain; yet that valley shall be filled with water, that ye may drink, both ye, and your cattle, and your beasts.

2 Kings 3:17

3. The Holy Spirit influenced Elisha to minister to widows.

And he said, About this season, according to the time of life, thou shalt embrace a son. And she said, Nay, my lord, thou man of God, do not lie unto thine handmaid.

And the woman conceived, and bare a son at that season that Elisha had said unto her, according to the time of life.

2 Kings 4:16-17

4. The Holy Spirit influenced Elisha to part the water.

And he took the mantle of Elijah that fell from him, and smote the waters, and said, Where is the LORD God of Elijah? and when he also had smitten the waters, they parted hither and thither: and Elisha went over.

2 Kings 2:14

CHAPTER 13

The Sweet Influences of the Anointing on Your Ministry Emphases

But ye shall receive power, AFTER THAT THE HOLY GHOST is come upon you: and YE SHALL BE WITNESSES UNTO ME both in Jerusalem, and in all Judaea, and in Samaria, and unto the uttermost part of the earth.

Acts 1:8

Ministers of the gospel emphasize different things. You only have to turn on your TV to discover the different things we all emphasize. Where do all these different emphases come from and what inspires them?

The Scripture above reveals that when the Holy Spirit comes on believers they are influenced to become witnesses to the rest of the world. When the Holy Spirit comes upon you, you will be influenced to emphasize soul winning, witnessing and evangelism. The Holy Spirit has not changed! God has not changed! And Jesus has not changed! When the Holy Spirit fell on the early church, the result was that they became witnesses to the whole world! If that same spirit falls on the Christian church today, the result will be that they will become witnesses to the whole world.

One may ask, "Which spirit has fallen on the church today?" It is a spirit that has made the church inward looking, money minded and materialistic! Is that the Holy Spirit? I do not think so! Because when the Holy Spirit fell on the early church, it made them leave everything behind and go to the whole world for the gospel's sake.

I think that the spirit that dominates the congregation is the spirit of the world and not the Holy Spirit. The spirit of the world drives people to become more established in this world. It is the spirit that drives the materialistic preaching and teaching of today. If you come under the influence of the Holy Spirit you will not be worldly and you will not be materialistic.

Now we have received, not THE SPIRIT OF THE WORLD, but the spirit which is of God; that we might know the things that are freely given to us of God.

1 Corinthians 2:12

I also think that the spirit that dominates many of us ministers is the spirit of Balaam. The spirit of Balaam is a common kind of anointing found in ministers today. It is a baffling mixture of spiritual gifts and the love of money. These ministers have wonderful genuine gifts that draw crowds and bless many thousands. Amazingly, these heavily gifted persons also have an easy-to-see love for money, popularity and power.

The influence of the spirit of Balaam and the influence of the spirit of the world have replaced the influence of the Holy Spirit in the church today. This is easy to see from the emphases that our ministries have. Pray for the influence of the Holy Spirit on your life and ministry.

CHAPTER 14

The Sweet Influences of the Holy Spirit on the Eyes of Your Heart

That the God of our Lord Jesus Christ, the Father of glory, may give to you a spirit of wisdom and of revelation in the knowledge of Him.

I pray that THE EYES OF YOUR HEART may be enlightened, so that you may know what is the hope of His calling, what are the riches of the glory of His inheritance in the saints, and what is the surpassing greatness of His power toward us who believe...

Ephesians 1:17-19, NASB

There is such a thing as "the eyes of the heart"! Your heart or your spirit has eyes. It is these eyes that have the ability to see spiritual things like visions and dreams. When your spiritual eyes are closed you never have any dreams or visions. But when they are opened, you experience visions for your life, visions of direction and important dreams that guide you in your ministry.

One of the most immediate effects of the presence of the Holy Spirit is visions and dreams. Remember that it is the direct prophecy of the prophet Joel that dreams and visions would begin with the Holy Spirit. Let us look at five powerful effects of the Holy Spirit on the eyes of your heart. The Scripture proves that all these effects on the eyes of your heart are direct influences of the Holy Spirit.

1. Under the sweet influences of the Holy Spirit, your eyes will see your true condition.

I counsel thee to buy of me gold tried in the fire, that thou mayest be rich; and white raiment, that thou mayest be clothed, and that the shame of thy nakedness do not appear; and ANOINT THINE EYES with eyesalve, that thou mayest see.

Revelation 3:18

When your eyes are not anointed, you have delusions about who you are and about how great you are. When the eyes of your heart are anointed by the influences of the Spirit, you will see your state of nakedness.

You will not call yourself rich when you are actually poor and desolate. Under the influence of the spirit of pride, you will never see wrong in yourself. When you are under the influence of evil spirits you will constantly argue about how right you are.

But when the Holy Spirit is upon you, He will reveal to you your true state of wretchedness.

Begin to ask for anointed eyes so that you see and know the truth about yourself. It is easy for me to pick out people with evil spirits who never agree that they have done something wrong. It is easy for a spiritual person to see the evil spirits in people who never yield, never agree, never say yes, never say no, never bow, never flow and never understand anything.

2. The sweet influences of the Holy Spirit on the eyes of your heart will cause you to see visions of the hope of your calling.

Under the influence of the Spirit, you have visions of the hope of your calling. You will have visions of the spiritual riches of glory that you possess. You also know the greatness of the power of God that is released towards you.

When *the spirit of the world* is upon you, you have visions of your hopes in the world of business and riches. When the spirit of the world is upon you, you have visions of the earthly riches that you could have. You are filled with the desire for earthly power. Pray that you will be under the sweet influence of the Holy Spirit.

3. The sweet influences of the Holy Spirit on the eyes of your heart will cause you to have meaningful dreams.

And it shall come to pass in the last days, saith God, I will POUR OUT OF MY SPIRIT upon all flesh: and your sons and your daughters shall prophesy, and your YOUNG MEN SHALL SEE VISIONS, and your old men shall dream dreams:

And on my servants and on my handmaidens I will pour out in those days of my Spirit; and they shall prophesy:

Acts 2:17-18

When you are not anointed by the Holy Spirit you will not dream. Even if you do dream, your dream will come from a multitude of business. "For a dream cometh through the multitude of business; and a fool's voice is known by multitude of words" (Ecclesiastes 5:3).

According to the Bible, when people received the Holy Spirit they began to have dreams. This is why dreaming is considered to be an ability that comes from the anointing. God has always spoken to men through dreams.

Through the influence of the Holy Spirit, God will do His greatest acts of mercy in your life. The greatest act of mercy in this world came through the dreams of Joseph. Expect great acts of mercy to come into your life through the influence of the Holy Spirit. There will be a surge of blessings into your life as the Holy Spirit influences you.

The birth of Jesus Christ and the supernatural guidance of Joseph came through the influence of the Holy Spirit. Through the Holy Spirit's influence, you will have dreams that will give direction to your life.

Without the influence of the spirit you will never have dreams, you will never have visions and you will never have direction! Without visions you will miss the direction of the Lord! How dangerous!

4. The sweet influences of the Holy Spirit on the eyes of your heart will cause you to interpret dreams.

But at the last Daniel came in before me, whose name was Belteshazzar, according to the name of my god, and in whom is the spirit of the holy gods: and before him I told the dream, saying,

O Belteshazzar, master of the magicians, because I know that THE SPIRIT OF THE HOLY GODS IS IN THEE, and no secret troubleth thee, tell me the visions of my dream that I have seen, and the interpretation thereof.

Daniel 4:8-9

Daniel understood dreams because of the influence of the Holy Spirit on his life. The unbelieving king Nebuchadnezzar knew that Daniel would be able to understand the dreams because of a spirit that Daniel seemed to have. Nebuchadnezzar did not know about the Holy Spirit but he knew that there was a spirit that influenced Daniel, enabling him to interpret visions and dreams. Since he did not know the sweet Holy Spirit he called Him *the spirit of the gods*!

5. **The sweet influences of the Holy Spirit on the eyes of your heart will cause you to start having visions just as Ezekiel did.**

Afterwards the spirit took me up, and brought me in A VISION BY THE SPIRIT OF GOD into Chaldea, to them of the captivity. So the vision that I had seen went up from me.

Ezekiel 11:24

6. **Under the sweet influences of the Holy Spirit, you will not despise the things you see with the eyes of your heart.**

Quench not the Spirit.

1 Thessalonians 5:19

Under the influence of the Holy Spirit, you will not despise the Holy Spirit's dreams. Show respect to the Holy Spirit by writing down the dreams and visions immediately. Show respect to the Holy Spirit by writing your dreams down immediately. Do not disregard even the smallest kind of dream or vision.

Jeremiah's first vision was to see a rod. The second one was to see a boiling pot. Most people would have despised such silly visions as being a figment of the imagination "Moreover the word of the Lord came unto me, saying, Jeremiah, what seest thou? And I said, I see a rod of an almond tree. Then said the Lord unto me, Thou hast well seen: for I will hasten my word to perform it" (Jeremiah 1:11-12). Under the influence of the Holy Spirit, Jeremiah believed there was something important about this mini vision.

Be open to the fact that you will make mistakes with your dreams and visions. Not everything will be accurate and not everything will be right. It is difficult to accept that some of your dreams and visions are actually mistakes.

Prove all things; hold fast that which is good.

1 Thessalonians 5:21

CHAPTER 15

The Sweet Influences of the Holy Spirit on Your Words

In the Christian world, we call inspired speeches "prophetic words". Prophecy is when a person speaks under inspiration.

Without the influence of the Holy Spirit you will be dull and uninteresting. Your boring lectures will put everyone to sleep and your listeners will pray earnestly for the end of your sermon. They will long to be away from your presence because you are neither inspired nor exciting.

It is only the Holy Spirit that can give you the inspiration you need. Under the sweet influences of the Holy Spirit, you will be inspired to teach, to preach and to live in the will of God.

How we need the sweet influence of the Holy Spirit! Without the sweet influences of the Holy Spirit, our speech will be under the inspiration of earthly ideas.

Ask for the Holy Spirit. Pray for the Holy Spirit. You will be inspired. Your words will not be rejected. People will not sleep when you are speaking. Men will change when they listen to your inspired words.

Most people speak under the inspiration of other spirits. They may speak from an earthly, sensual or devilish inspiration. But you need to be under the sweet influence of the Holy Spirit.

Without the sweet influence of the Holy Spirit, you may be in danger of speaking under the devilish inspiration of bitterness, jealousy or hatred.

Many politicians speak under a demonic influence and inspiration. They incite war, revenge and hatred through their demonic and dark speeches. Read about Rwanda and you will discover how the demonic influences on leaders inspired the mass murder. If you listen to the speeches of Hitler, you hear the voice of Satan over and over again. Hitler's henchmen were equally filled with the spirit of Satan. You see and sense evil, wickedness, deception, cruelty, mercilessness, retaliation and murder in their very words. Which spirit is inspiring your messages?

1. **When servants and handmaidens came under the sweet influence of the Holy Spirit, they began to prophesy and speak under inspiration.**

   And it shall come to pass in the last days, saith God, I will pour out of MY SPIRIT upon all flesh: and YOUR SONS AND YOUR DAUGHTERS SHALL PROPHESY, and your young men shall see visions, and your old men shall dream dreams:
   And on my servants and on my handmaidens I will pour out in those days of my Spirit; and THEY SHALL PROPHESY:

   Acts 2:17-18

2. **When the disciples in Ephesus came under the sweet influence of the Holy Spirit they became inspired and prophesied.**

   And when Paul had laid his hands upon them, THE HOLY GHOST CAME on them; and they spake with tongues, and PROPHESIED. And all the men were about twelve.

   Acts 19:6-7

3. **When Zacharias came under the sweet influence of the Holy Spirit he began to prophesy and speak wonderful words that have been written down for thousands of years.**

And his father ZACHARIAS WAS FILLED WITH THE HOLY GHOST, AND PROPHESIED, saying, Blessed be the Lord God of Israel; for he hath visited and redeemed his people,

And hath raised up an horn of salvation for us in the house of his servant David;

Luke 1:67-69

4. **When Jahaziel, son of Zechariah, came under the sweet influence of the Holy Spirit,he spoke words that inspired the Israelites to rise up and fight for God.**

Then UPON JAHAZIEL the son of Zechariah, the son of Benaiah, the son of Jeiel, the son of Mattaniah, a Levite of the sons of Asaph, CAME THE SPIRIT OF THE LORD in the midst of the congregation;

And he said, Hearken ye, all Judah, and ye inhabitants of Jerusalem, and thou king Jehoshaphat, Thus saith the LORD unto you, Be not afraid nor dismayed by reason of this great multitude; for the battle is not yours, but God's.

To morrow go ye down against them: behold, they come up by the cliff of Ziz; and ye shall find them at the end of the brook, before the wilderness of Jeruel.

Ye shall not need to fight in this battle: set yourselves, stand ye still, and see the salvation of the LORD with you, O Judah and Jerusalem: fear not, nor be dismayed; to morrow go out against them: for the LORD will be with you.

2 Chronicles 20:14-17

CHAPTER 16

The Sweet Influences of the Holy Spirit on Your Charisma

Charisma means gracefulness and beauty. Through the influence of the Holy Spirit you become charismatic. That means you become graceful and beautiful. Do you want to be graceful? Do you want to be beautiful? Do you want to attract the people God has called? Then you must come under the influence of the Holy Spirit and become charismatic.

Charis means grace.

Charisma means manifestation of grace.

Charismata means multiple manifestations of grace.

A charismatic person is a gifted and inspired person. He receives multiple manifestations of gracefulness and beauty. This makes him have a magnetic appeal. It is this magnetic appeal that draws people to listen to him. The Holy Spirit causes people to be drawn to help and support a charismatic person.

When you are a servant of the Lord, it is the influence of the spirit that makes you attractive. It is not your looks, your dressing, your education or how tall you are that draws people to you. It is the influence of the Holy Spirit that makes you attractive and makes people want to listen to you.

In the ministry, it is your giftedness that attracts the masses. Most people are not gifted and have nothing to offer. The Holy Spirit is the bringer of gifts. Several gifts come to you when you are under the influence of the Spirit. They are sometimes called manifestations. It is these different multiple manifestations of the Holy Spirit that make you graceful and beautiful.

1. When a minister comes under the sweet influence of the Holy Spirit he has various manifestations of gifts in his life.

But the MANIFESTATION OF THE SPIRIT is given to every man to profit withal. For TO ONE IS GIVEN BY THE SPIRIT the word of wisdom; to another the word of knowledge by the same Spirit; To another faith by the same Spirit; to another the gifts of healing by the same Spirit; To another the working of miracles; to another prophecy; to another discerning of spirits; to another divers kinds of tongues; to another the interpretation of tongues: But all these worketh that one and the selfsame Spirit, dividing to every man severally as he will.

1 Corinthians 12:7-11

2. When a minister comes under the sweet influence of the Holy Spirit he has supernatural wisdom.

The officers answered, Never man spake like this man.

John 7:46

3. When a minister comes under the sweet influence of the Holy Spirit he has supernatural knowledge.

Jesus saith unto her, Go, call thy husband, and come hither The woman answered and said, I have no husband. Jesus said unto her, Thou hast well said, I have no husband: For thou hast had five husbands; and he whom thou now hast is not thy husband: in that saidst thou truly. The woman saith unto him, Sir, I perceive that thou art a prophet.

John 4:16-19

4. **When a minister comes under the sweet influence of the Holy Spirit he has a supernatural ability to discern spirits.**

But when he had turned about and looked on his disciples, he rebuked Peter, saying, Get thee behind me, Satan: for thou savourest not the things that be of God, but the things that be of men.

Mark 8:33

5. **When a minister comes under the sweet influence of the Holy Spirit he has a supernatural ability to exercise faith.**

But as they sailed he fell asleep: and there came down a storm of wind on the lake; and they were filled with water, and were in jeopardy.

And they came to him, and awoke him, saying, Master, master, we perish. Then he arose, and rebuked the wind and the raging of the water: and they ceased, and there was a calm.

Luke 8:23-24

6. **When a minister comes under the sweet influence of the Holy Spirit he has a supernatural gift of healing.**

Now when he came nigh to the gate of the city, behold, there was a dead man carried out, the only son of his mother, and she was a widow: and much people of the city was with her.
And when the Lord saw her, he had compassion on her, and said unto her, Weep not.
And he came and touched the bier: and they that bare him stood still. And he said, Young man, I say unto thee, Arise. And he that was dead sat up, and began to speak. And he delivered him to his mother.

Luke 7:12-15

7. **When a minister comes under the sweet influence of the Holy Spirit he has supernatural ability to speak in tongues and to interpret tongues.**

CHAPTER 17

The Sweet Influences of the Holy Spirit to Assure You

Now he which stablisheth us with you in Christ, and hath anointed us, is God; Who hath also sealed us, and given the EARNEST OF THE SPIRIT in our hearts.

2 Corinthians 1:21-22

1. God assures you of His approval by the Holy Spirit's presence.

The Holy Spirit's presence in your life is a guarantee and a further assurance of His approval on your life. Read it for yourself: The presence of the Holy Spirit is the guarantee, the seal, the pledge and the assurance that you need. God has left the Holy Spirit in our midst so that He is present in all that we do. His presence is supposed to assure us and calm us down. His presence is supposed to be a guarantee that assures us in what we do. "Now he that hath wrought us for the selfsame thing is God, who also hath given unto us the EARNEST OF THE SPIRIT" (2 Corinthians 5:5).

Are you approved? Does God like you? Is God happy with you? Is He happy with your songs? Does God agree with all that you are doing? You need some assurance, don't you? That assurance comes from the presence of the Holy Spirit. The influence of the Holy Spirit will calm and reassure you when you are uncertain about whether you are walking in His will.

Why does your financial prosperity give you assurance? Where did you read that? Where do you learn these things? Are you now being tutored by the world's system? How come you are looking at your financial status, your new job, your car and your house to give you an assurance that God is with you? When did these things become your guarantee? The Holy Spirit is the guarantee and not any earthly possession.

It is because you are a carnal man operating under an earthly influence that earthly things are assuring you of God's love for you. It is secular businessmen who are assured and encouraged by their bank balances and financial incomes. You, as a spiritual person, must be assured by the presence of the Holy Spirit.

Your convictions must be strengthened by the presence of God. The presence of the Holy Spirit must be your source of assurance. This is one of the most important functions of the Holy Spirit; to assure you.

Over and over, the Holy Spirit is called an earnest pledge or a guarantee. He guarantees that you are on the right way by His presence. You must always look for the presence of the Holy Spirit.

Moses would not go one step forward without the guarantee of the presence of the Lord. You must become like Moses who looked for guarantees and assurances in the presence of the Lord.

> Then he said to Him, "If Thy presence does not go with us, do not lead us up from here.
>
> For how then can it be known that I have found favor in Thy sight, I and Thy people? Is it not by Thy going with us, so that we, I and Thy people, may be distinguished from all the other people who are upon the face of the earth?
>
> Exodus 33:15-16 (NASB)

2. Under the influence of the Holy Spirit you develop convictions and assurances.

> And because ye are sons, God hath sent forth the Spirit of his Son into your hearts, crying, Abba, Father.
>
> Galatians 4:6

The Holy Spirit influences your convictions by crying out about certain things in your heart.

Anyone who is under the sweet influence of the Holy Spirit will become sure of certain realities because the Holy Spirit will cry and repeatedly speak certain words in your heart. These words that the Holy Spirit speaks in your heart will become convictions that you hold onto. You will be sure of these things without having reasons why.

Are you beginning to form certain convictions in your heart? Are you becoming sure about certain things? Is there a mysterious knowing in your heart? Is your soul mystically longing for certain things? Are certain spiritual desires growing and developing in you? Is your heart crying for certain things? These are all mystical works of the Holy Spirit.

CHAPTER 18

The Sweet Influences of the Holy Spirit on Your Level of Obedience

Moreover, I will give you a new heart and put a new spirit within you; and I will remove the heart of stone from your flesh and give you a heart of flesh.

And I WILL PUT MY SPIRIT WITHIN YOU AND CAUSE YOU TO WALK IN MY STATUTES, and you will be careful to observe My ordinances.

Ezekiel 36:26-27 (NASB)

Amazingly, it is the Holy Spirit who helps us to obey the commandments of the Lord. When someone is under the influence of the Spirit of the Lord, it becomes easy for him to obey the commandments of the Lord. The very one who gives you the instruction, sends His Spirit to cause you to be obedient. This is why none of us should boast in ourselves. Whatever we are able to do has been given to us by the Holy Spirit.

Do you want to obey God? Do you love God? Are you struggling to be obedient to the commandments of God?

Pray to God for the Holy Spirit and you will have the ability to obey Him. He Himself will make you walk in obedience. Do not trust in your own abilities. Bring yourself under the beautiful influence of the Holy Spirit right now.

CHAPTER 19

The Sweet Influences of the Holy Spirit on Your Level of Boldness

And when they had prayed, the place was shaken where they were assembled together; and they were all FILLED WITH THE HOLY GHOST, AND THEY SPAKE THE WORD OF GOD WITH BOLDNESS.

Acts 4:31

O ne of the most amazing effects of the influence of the Holy Spirit will be the dramatic change in your level of boldness.

Frightened, timid and disillusioned apostles hiding in a room were transformed instantly into a bold and fearless team of preachers. They seemed to have no fears any more. They suddenly seemed to know how to give speeches in public. They faced up to the murderers of Christ boldly and preached confrontational sermons! You can contrast this with Peter's vehement denial of Christ a few days before. What caused such drastic changes? The Holy Spirit! You need the Holy Spirit to grow in boldness in the ministry.

And they were all filled with the Holy Ghost, and began to speak with other tongues, as the Spirit gave them utterance . . .Peter, standing up with the eleven, lifted up his voice, and said unto them, Ye men of Judaea, and all ye that dwell at Jerusalem, be this known unto you, and hearken to my words:

For these are not drunken, as ye suppose, seeing it is but the third hour of the day.

Acts 2:4,14-15

Peter was emboldened by the influence of the Holy Spirit. All the apostles were emboldened and empowered by the influence of the Holy Spirit. Boldness is a key to the anointing. Boldness is a key to the presence of God. "Let us therefore come boldly unto the throne of grace, that we may obtain mercy, and find grace to help in time of need" (Hebrews 4:16). You will receive boldness for your ministry when the Holy Spirit comes upon you. Without boldness you cannot minister healing, miracles, signs and wonders. You need boldness to call out miracles. You need boldness to minister the Spirit. You need boldness to take certain steps that will bring down the presence of God. It is the sweet influence of the Holy Spirit that makes you bolder and bolder.

Under the Holy Spirit, you will become even more emboldened to minister power to all the hungry people of the world. Without boldness you cannot step into the Holy of Holies and into the presence of the anointing. The Word of God tells us to come boldly into His presence. Without boldness you are missing a major key to the presence of God.

CHAPTER 20

The Sweet Influences of the Holy Spirit on Your Marriage

Yet you say, 'For what reason?' Because the Lord has been a witness between you and the wife of your youth, against whom YOU HAVE DEALT TREACHEROUSLY, though SHE IS YOUR COMPANION and your wife by covenant.

BUT NOT ONE HAS DONE SO WHO HAS A REMNANT OF THE SPIRIT. And what did that one do while he was seeking a godly offspring? Take heed then, to your spirit, and let no one deal treacherously against the wife of your youth.

"For I hate divorce," says the Lord, the God of Israel, "and him who covers his garment with wrong," says the Lord of hosts. "So take heed to your spirit, that you do not deal treacherously."

Malachi 2:14-16 (NASB)

The influence of the Holy Spirit will cause you to hate divorce and love marriage. When other influences step in, divorce becomes a possibility. As the church has moved away from the Holy Spirit, divorce has become more and more common. Instead of following the Holy Spirit, most of the church is running after the world and its systems.

Our love for the world is so great and the evil spirits of the world have swarmed into the church, taking over our values and principles. Today, the prevalence of the spirit of the world has made it acceptable for us to divorce and remarry several times over.

But Malachi the prophet said, *people who have the remnant of the Holy Spirit have not done so.* What does this mean? Even those with a small portion (remnant) of the Holy Spirit will know that they have to resist divorce.

Let us return and walk under the influence of the Holy Spirit. Let us shun the spirits in the world. Let us come under the sweet influences of the Holy Spirit. Under the influence of the Holy Spirit, we will love marriage and hate divorce.

Do not allow anything or anyone to replace the Holy Spirit. Allow the Holy Spirit to influence your heart and lead you into His will. For sure, there are fantastically difficult marriages. Many marriages have desperate and chronic problems with no hope of change in sight! Yet we are faced with this mystical instruction to hate divorce and avoid it at all costs. We are warned that the people who are under the influence of the Spirit will not deal treacherously with their spouses.

Pray for the help of God! Pray that you may survive! Pray for the powerful influence of the Holy Spirit to come over your situation and help you to outmanoeuvre the demons and forces that are arraigned against your life, your marriage and your sanctity.

CHAPTER 21

The Sweet Influences of the Holy Spirit on Your Willingness and Eagerness

And they came, every one whose heart stirred him up, and every one WHOM HIS SPIRIT MADE WILLING, and they brought the Lord's offering to the work of the tabernacle of the congregation, and for all his service, and for the holy garments.

Exodus 35:21

Without the influence of the Holy Spirit most people grumble when they have to do something. They complain, they murmur, they go on strike and exhibit many different forms of discontentment. It is hard to find a workplace without discontented and grumbling employees. Such is the nature of man without the influence of the Holy Spirit.

Our churches are equally filled with discontented, grumbling and criticizing members. Most of these murmurers are filled with evil spirits like the complaining Israelites who followed Moses.

This is why we need the Holy Spirit to fill our churches. The Holy Spirit imparts a different attitude. The Holy Spirit imparts eagerness and willingness to people. Satan and his demonic hordes impart discontentment, criticism and accusations!

Willingness and eagerness are true spiritual qualities that come from the Holy Spirit.

When you are under the influence of the Holy Spirit you will be willing because the Holy Spirit makes you willing and eager. The children of Israel were willing to give offerings because the Holy Spirit had touched their hearts to make them willing givers. There is no need to coerce people to give money. God will touch their hearts and they will give when the Holy Spirit has made them willing.

> **But my servant Caleb, because HE HAD ANOTHER SPIRIT with him, and HATH FOLLOWED ME FULLY, him will I bring into the land whereinto he went; and his seed shall possess it.**
>
> **Numbers 14:24**

The Bible is clear about the source of Caleb's eagerness.

When you are under the influence of the Holy Spirit you will be willing and eager. Caleb was eager because he was under the influence of the Holy Spirit.

CHAPTER 22

The Sweet Influences of the Holy Spirit on Your Talents and Abilities

Three Special Abilities

1. The Holy Spirit imparts special abilities to individuals. Under the influence of the Holy Spirit, you will have certain special talents and abilities. Bezaleel is the best example of someone who came under the influence of the Spirit of God and received special abilities from God. The Holy Spirit gave him the ability to build the tabernacle and to design wonderful works for the Lord.

See, I have called by name Bezaleel the son of Uri, the son of Hur, of the tribe of Judah:

And I HAVE FILLED HIM WITH THE SPIRIT OF GOD, in wisdom, and in understanding, and in knowledge, and in all manner of workmanship,

TO DEVISE CUNNING WORKS, to work in gold, and in silver, and in brass,

And in cutting of stones, to set them, and in carving of timber, to work in all manner of workmanship,

Exodus 31:2-3

2.   Under the influence of the Holy Spirit, you can receive the ability to do almost anything. Tailors and seamstresses who came under the influence of the Holy Spirit were able to create the most elaborate and beautiful gowns for the priests. Many people with special talents have received these from the Holy Spirit.

And thou shalt speak unto all that are wise hearted, WHOM I HAVE FILLED WITH THE SPIRIT OF WISDOM, that they may MAKE AARON'S GARMENTS to consecrate him, that he may minister unto me in the priest's office.

Exodus 28:3

3.   Under the influence of the Holy Spirit you can receive the ability to govern and to create wealth.

And Pharaoh said unto his servants, can we find such a one as this is, A MAN IN WHOM THE SPIRIT OF GOD is?
And Pharaoh said unto Joseph, Forasmuch as God hath shewed thee all this, there is none so discreet and wise as thou art:
Thou shalt be over my house, and according unto thy word shall all my people be ruled: only in the throne will I be greater than thou.

Genesis 41:38-40

Through the influence of the Holy Spirit, you can receive the ability to create and sustain great riches. Pharaoh recognized that Joseph would have the ability to sustain and retain the wealth of Egypt.

Sometimes, people receive great wealth but lose everything because they receive the wealth from demons. The demons give them the wealth and then, the demons make them throw everything away again. You must remember how Satan told Jesus that all the wealth of the world was his to give. It is a clearly established fact that Satan also gives wealth to people.

Many people are given jobs by demons. These jobs seem to be the best thing in the world. But they end in disappointment and emptiness.

Why don't you pray for the Holy Spirit to come upon your life? Under the sweet influence of the Holy Spirit, you will create wealth and be able to retain it. There is a powerful influence of wealth creation that comes by the presence of the Holy Spirit. Oh how we need the influence of the Holy Spirit!

The Sweet Influences of the Holy Spirit on Your Creativity

And the earth was without form, and void; and darkness was upon the face of the deep. And THE SPIRIT OF GOD MOVED upon the face of the waters.

And God said, LET THERE BE LIGHT: and there was light.

Genesis 1:2-3

Creative people are influenced by the Holy Spirit to create and to invent. When the Holy Spirit moved, God the Father created the world. If the moving of the Holy Spirit brought about the creation of this world, then the moving of the Holy Spirit in your life will bring about creativity in your ministry. The greatest leaders of this world created and built new things. People rallied around their ideas and followed their creative ideas.

When a person is under the influence of the Holy Spirit, he becomes creative. The absence of the Holy Spirit leads to monotonous leadership that lacks ideas. God will use you to create new things and to do new things.

He will use you to name things that have no names. He will use you to build things that never existed before.

Allow the Holy Spirit to move in your life. Allow creative power to flow through you. Let creativity and innovation characterize your ministry and your life. Don't be dull and monotonous. Receive the Holy Spirit and the influence that comes from Him. Believe in new things and believe that the mystical presence of the Spirit is showing you new ways of doing old things. The creative power of God is flowing through you by the power of the Holy Spirit.

CHAPTER 24

The Sweet Influences of the Holy Spirit on Your Productivity

Until THE SPIRIT be poured upon us from on high, and THE WILDERNESS BE A FRUITFUL FIELD, and the fruitful field be counted for a forest.

Isaiah 32:15

Notice the Scripture above. The wilderness is turned into a fruitful field and a fruitful field is converted into a forest by the Holy Spirit.

The presence of the Holy Spirit influences your fruitfulness. Many people attribute productivity and fruitfulness to natural causes and reasons. But the truth is that the Holy Spirit is the one who makes you productive.

What a change! What an improvement! What fruitfulness and what productivity all because of the presence of the Holy Spirit. My attempts at being a farmer have revealed to me that no one can be fruitful and productive unless God blesses him. The multiplying herds of Abraham, Isaac and Jacob can only be attributed to the influence of the presence of the Holy Spirit. The presence of the Holy Spirit turns the wilderness into a fruitful field.

You can choose what you believe. I prefer to pray for the influence of the Holy Spirit. He will give me fruits on my branches. He will give me fruits. Paul may have planted and Apollos may have watered, but God (the Holy Spirit) gave the increase.

CHAPTER 25

The Sweet Influences of the Holy Spirit on Your Accomplishments

… for without me ye can do nothing.

John 15:5

It is God's power that enables you to accomplish great things for Him. Without the Holy Spirit you cannot do anything. All through the Bible you see examples of people doing great things for God. All these things were done under the influence of the Holy Spirit.

Do you want to do great things for God? It will come about through the influence of the Holy Spirit. Let us look at how the Holy Spirit influenced different people to accomplish great things for Him.

1. Through the sweet influence of the Holy Spirit you will deliver people from their enemies.

And when the children of Israel cried unto the LORD, the LORD raised up a deliverer to the children of Israel who delivered them, even OTHNIEL the son of Kenaz, Caleb's younger brother.

And THE SPIRIT OF THE LORD CAME UPON HIM, and he judged Israel, and went out to war: and the LORD delivered Chushanrishathaim king of Mesopotamia into his hand; and HIS HAND PREVAILED AGAINST CHUSHANRISHATHAIM.

Judges 3:9-10

The sweet influence of the Holy Spirit upon Othniel enabled him to deliver the people of God in war. Othniel overcame his enemy Chushanrishathaim by the power and influence of the Holy Spirit.

2. Through the sweet influence of the Holy Spirit you will gather many people together for a good cause.

Then all the Midianites and the Amalekites and the children of the east were gathered together, and went over, and pitched in the valley of Jezreel.

But the SPIRIT OF THE LORD CAME UPON GIDEON, and he blew a trumpet; and ABIEZER WAS GATHERED after him.

Judges 6:33-34

With the power of the Holy Spirit, men gathered around Gideon to help him fight the war. Have you wondered why people are not gathering to listen to you in your church? When the influence of the Holy Spirit in your life is stronger than the influence of the spirit of the world, men will gather to hear what you have to say.

3. Through the sweet influence of the Holy Spirit you will have supernatural strength for great accomplishments.

Samson had supernatural strength when the Spirit of the Lord came upon him. He killed lions, he tore chains and killed many men at the same time.
And the SPIRIT OF THE LORD CAME mightily upon him, and HE RENT HIM as he would have rent a kid, and he had nothing in his hand: but he told not his father or his mother what he had done.

Judges 14:6

And the SPIRIT OF THE LORD CAME upon him, and he went down to Ashkelon, and SLEW THIRTY MEN of them, and took their spoil, and gave change of garments unto them which expounded the riddle. And his anger was kindled, and he went up to his father's house.

Judges 14:19

And when he came unto Lehi, the Philistines shouted against him: and the SPIRIT OF THE LORD CAME mightily upon him, and the cords that were upon his arms became as flax that was burnt with fire, and HIS BANDS LOOSED from off his hands.

Judges 15:14

4. Through the sweet influence of the Holy Spirit you will become a great leader.

Then Samuel took the horn of oil, and anointed him in the midst of his brethren: and THE SPIRIT OF THE LORD CAME UPON DAVID from that day forward. So Samuel rose up, and went to Ramah.

1 Samuel 16:13

When David came under the influence of the Holy Spirit he became a great king of Israel. Through the influence of the Holy Spirit you will become a great leader. Allow the Holy Spirit to influence you. He is turning you into a great king.

5. Through the sweet influence of the Holy Spirit your fear of confrontation will be gone.

And the SPIRIT OF GOD CAME UPON ZECHARIAH the son of Jehoiada the priest, which stood above the people, and said unto them, thus saith God, WHY TRANSGRESS YE the commandments of the Lord, that ye cannot prosper? Because ye have forsaken the Lord, he hath also forsaken you.

2 Chronicles 24:20

You will be able to confront people who are walking in sin. Zechariah was under the influence of the Holy Spirit. That is why he was able to rebuke the people about their sins. If the Holy Spirit has left you, you will stop speaking about sin and confronting the evil in the church.

6. Through the sweet influence of the Holy Spirit you will become a builder of the house of God.

Then he answered and spake unto me, saying, this is the word of the Lord unto Zerubbabel, saying, not by might, nor by power, but BY MY SPIRIT, saith the Lord of hosts.

Who art thou, O great mountain? Before Zerubbabel thou shalt become a plain: and he shall bring forth the headstone thereof with shoutings, crying, Grace, grace unto it.

Moreover the word of the Lord came unto me, saying,

The hands of Zerubbabel have laid the foundation of this house; HIS HANDS SHALL ALSO FINISH IT; and thou shalt know that the Lord of hosts hath sent me unto you.

Zechariah 4:6-9

People who are not under the influence of the Holy Spirit cannot build anything for God. Under the sweet influence of the Holy Spirit, Zerubbabel became a builder of the house of

God. The Holy Spirit will also influence you to finish whatever you have started. Under the influence of the Holy Spirit you will overcome financial obstacles and great mountains. It is only under the influence of the Holy Spirit that you can accomplish great things.

7. Through the sweet influence of the Holy Spirit your personality will be transformed.

And THE SPIRIT of the LORD WILL COME upon thee, and thou shalt prophesy with them, and SHALT BE TURNED INTO ANOTHER MAN.

1 Samuel 10:6

Saul was transformed into another man when he came under the sweet influence of the Holy Spirit. Watch yourself carefully. You will notice how you are changing under the influence of the Holy Spirit. Don't resist the changes that the Holy Spirit is bringing to your life. You are under the influence of the Holy Spirit and He is changing you completely!

8. Through the sweet influence of the Holy Spirit you will go out to war and fight the good fight of faith.

So the SPIRIT OF THE LORD came upon Gideon; and he BLEW A TRUMPET, and the Abiezrites were called together to follow him.

And he sent messengers throughout Manasseh, and they also were called together to follow him; and he sent messengers to Asher, Zebulun, and Naphtali, and they came up to meet them.

Judges 6:34-35 (NASB)

When you are under the influence of the Holy Spirit, you are charged up to fight for the Lord. People who are not motivated to do the work of the Lord are not under the influence of the Holy Spirit. People who love to rest, to sleep and to do nothing when the world is lost and going to Hell are not under the influence of the Holy Spirit.

When you are under the influence of the Holy Spirit you will rise up and blow a trumpet so that the children of God gather together for the war. Paul, under the influence of the Holy Spirit, told Timothy to wage a good warfare! When you are under the influence of a lazy personality, you will tell the people to go home and rest.

9. Through the sweet influence of the Holy Spirit you will heal the sick and cast out devils.

The Spirit of the Lord is upon me, because he hath anointed me to preach the gospel to the poor; he hath sent me to heal the brokenhearted, to preach deliverance to the captives, and recovering of sight to the blind, to set at liberty them that are bruised

Luke 4:18

Initially, Jesus did not heal the sick or preach the gospel to anyone. He simply worked as a carpenter. He was known as a faithful and religious man. But when the Spirit of the Lord came upon Him after His experience in the Jordan River, He changed drastically. He came under the sweet influences of the Holy Spirit and began to preach the gospel, to heal the sick and to cast out devils. What a vast difference the Holy Spirit makes in your life! Bow down and come under the influence of the Holy Spirit. Your ministry needs this influence. You need signs and wonders, miracles and healings. These are the mighty works of God that come when a minister is under the influence of the Holy Spirit.

The Sweet Influences of the Holy Spirit on Your Calling and Destiny

And the Spirit and the bride say, COME.

Revelation 22:17

Be sure to obey the call of God because the call of God comes from the Holy Spirit. *It is the Spirit that is saying that you must come and serve Him!* All things work together for good for those who are called. All things do not work together for good for everyone. God has determined that all things will work together for good for those who are called. As you obey the call of God you will experience the blessings of a "called" person. Allow yourself to hear the Holy Spirit saying, "come".

Five Blessings of Responding to the Call and Influence of the Spirit

1. *Foreknew:* God knows about you before He calls and elects you.

    ELECT according to the FOREKNOWLEDGE of God the Father, through sanctification of the Spirit, unto obedience and sprinkling of the blood of Jesus Christ: Grace unto you, and peace, be multiplied.

    1 Peter 1:2

2. *Predestined:* God had planned that He would make you like Him.

    For whom he did foreknow, he also did PREDESTINATE TO BE CONFORMED to the image of his Son, that he might be the firstborn among many brethren.

    Romans 8:29

3. *Called:* it is only after God has done background checks on you and has planned a great destiny for your future that He actually calls you. To reject the call of God is to reject all the special treatment and privileges God has lined up for you.

    Moreover whom he did predestinate, them HE ALSO CALLED: and whom he called, them he also justified: and whom he justified, them he also glorified.

    Romans 8:30

4. *Justified:* This calling has amazing implications. Those who accept the call are justified. They are made right with God for accepting the call. They are not made right for their good deeds. Accepting the call and responding to it is one of the greatest acts of righteousness. That is why God justifies those who are called. What an honour it is to be called! What a privilege! What grace has abounded to your life because you are called!

Moreover whom he did predestinate, them he also called: and whom he called, them HE ALSO JUSTIFIED: and whom he justified, them he also glorified.

Romans 8:30

5. *Glorified:* There are even more unexpected blessings of the call. After being justified and being declared righteous, God has plans to glorify you. Just because you accepted the call! Imagine that! Who would have thought that accepting the call would lead to justification and even glorification? What a shock! What a blessing it is to respond to the influences of the Holy Spirit!

Moreover whom he did predestinate, them he also called: and whom he called, them he also justified: and whom he justified, them HE ALSO GLORIFIED.

Romans 8:30

CHAPTER 27

The Sweet Influences of the Holy Spirit on Your Level of Honesty

1. **A person under the sweet influence of the Holy Spirit will love the truth and dislike lies and dishonesty.**

   Even THE SPIRIT OF TRUTH; whom the world cannot receive, because it seeth him not, neither knoweth him: but ye know him; for he dwelleth with you, and shall be in you.

   John 14:17

   This is because the Holy Spirit is the spirit of truth and the spirit of light. The more the Holy Spirit is in you, the more the darkness of dishonesty will be put far away from you. When a person freely tells lies you can be sure he is not under the influence of the Holy Spirit. Lies and dishonesty are a revelation of the presence of evil spirits in people.

2. **A person under the sweet influence of the Holy Spirit becomes honest. Stephen was honest because he was full of the Holy Ghost.**

   Wherefore, brethren, look ye out among you seven MEN OF HONEST REPORT, FULL OF THE HOLY GHOST and wisdom, whom we may appoint over this business ...

And the saying pleased the whole multitude: and they chose Stephen, a man full of faith and of the Holy Ghost, and Philip, and Prochorus, and Nicanor, and Timon, and Parmenas, and Nicolas a proselyte of Antioch:

Acts 6:3,5

3. **A person under the sweet influence of the Holy Spirit will detect falsehood, deception, deceit and dishonesty.**

Then Peter said unto her, how is it that ye have agreed together to tempt the Spirit of the Lord? Behold, the feet of them which have buried thy husband are at the door, and shall carry thee out.

Acts 5:9

These evils do not thrive in the presence of the Holy Spirit. The sweet influence of the Holy Spirit removes all these spots of deception from our midst. The Holy Spirit could not stand the lies and deception of Ananias and Sapphira. The Holy Spirit is the spirit of truth. Ananias and Sapphira paid a high price for bringing dishonesty and deception into the presence of the Holy Spirit.

CHAPTER 28

The Sweet Influences of the Holy Spirit Give You Life

1. **The sweet influence of the Holy Spirit brings life because He is the spirit of life.** The more you have the Holy Spirit in you, the more alive and lively you will be.

   For the law of THE SPIRIT OF LIFE in Christ Jesus hath made me free from the law of sin and death.

   Romans 8:2

2. **The sweet influence of the Holy Spirit gives you the very life that you have on this earth.** The sweet influence of the Holy Spirit extends your life on this earth because He is the spirit of life. Do you want to live long? Pray for the Holy Spirit to fill you and guide you.

   And the LORD God formed man of the dust of the ground, and breathed into his nostrils THE BREATH OF LIFE; and man became a living soul.

   Genesis 2:7

   And after three days and an half THE SPIRIT OF LIFE FROM GOD ENTERED into them, and they stood upon their feet; and great fear fell upon them which saw them.

   Revelation 11:11

3. The sweet influence of the Holy Spirit guides you to everlasting life.

For he that soweth to his flesh shall of the flesh reap corruption; but he that soweth to the Spirit shall OF THE SPIRIT REAP LIFE EVERLASTING.

Galatians 6:8

CHAPTER 29

The Sweet Influences of the Holy Spirit on Your Becoming a Pastor

Take heed therefore unto yourselves, and to all the flock, over the which THE HOLY GHOST HATH MADE YOU OVERSEERS, to feed the church of God, which he hath purchased with his own blood.

Acts 20:28

It is easy to see from the Scripture above that the Holy Spirit makes people overseers. The Holy Spirit wants to make you into a pastor. When you come under the influence of the Holy Spirit, you will sense a calling to become a pastor.

An overseer cannot be made by man. A minister of the gospel is someone who is called, anointed and clothed by God Himself. Man-made ministers, who fill the pulpits of many churches, are often leading people to Hell. Do not follow an overseer who was not "made" by the Holy Spirit!

Also, do not enter the ministry unless the Holy Spirit has made you an overseer. It is the Holy Spirit who "makes" overseers.

CHAPTER 30

The Sweet Influences of the Holy Spirit on Your Relationship with the Body of Christ

1. **When you are under the influence of the Holy Spirit, you will not separate yourself.**

These be they who SEPARATE themselves, sensual, HAVING NOT THE SPIRIT.

Jude 19

Time and time again, I have watched helplessly as evil spirits led dearly loved brethren away from the fold. People, who should have known better, followed demons as they led them out of the church. The Holy Spirit will influence you not to be separated from the rest of the brethren. It is demons who influence people to separate themselves from the rest of the body. The Holy Spirit does the exact opposite of that. If you remember this, you will react properly to every attempt to ever separate you from your spiritual family. I would prefer to live my life without ever following a demon. Do not follow a demon, not even for a day!

2. When you are under the influence of the Holy Spirit, you will unite with other Christians.

Endeavouring to keep the UNITY OF THE SPIRIT in the bond of peace.

Ephesians 4:3

The Holy Spirit will influence you to be united with the rest of the body of Christ. Unity in the church is actually called "unity of the Holy Spirit". Unity is brought about by a direct influence of the Holy Spirit.

The world we live in is opposed to unity. Hurts and offences that are in the world constantly work to divide us and break vital relationships. It is only by the power of the Holy Spirit that we can continue to stay together. The Holy Spirit does not inspire isolation and living lonely lives. The Holy Spirit inspires you to be with the others and to stay within the fellowship.

CHAPTER 31

How to Stir Up the Sweet Influence of the Holy Spirit

... that thou stir up the gift of God. . .

2 Timothy 1:6

1. **Stir up interest and hunger in the Holy Spirit by talking and preaching about the Holy Spirit.**

> Blessed are they which do hunger and thirst after righteousness: for they shall be filled.
>
> Matthew 5:6

You can stir up interest in anything by talking about it. Have you noticed that you become hungry when you talk about food? Have you noticed that when you talk about America your interest in America increases? Have you noticed that your interest in sex increases as you talk about it? When pastors preach about money, prosperity and finances, their congregation develops an interest and hunger for money. The reason why modern churches are filled with many greedy, covetous and money-loving Christians is because we the pastors are constantly teaching on how and why you must be rich!

Similarly, talking about the Holy Spirit stirs up a hunger and interest in the things of the Spirit. Do not be surprised when there are manifestations of the Spirit in ministries that preach and teach about the Holy Spirit. They are stirring up interest in the Holy Spirit when they talk about the Holy Spirit, His gifts and His manifestations.

Do you want manifestations of the Holy Spirit? Do you want the sweet influences of the Holy Spirit to increase in your life? Then start talking and preaching about it! You will create a genuine hunger for these things. The hunger you create will result in the blessing of being filled. The blessing of being hungry is that you will be filled with the Holy Spirit.

2. **Stir up the sweet influences of the Holy Spirit by praying specifically for the Holy Spirit.**

> If ye then, being evil, know how to give good gifts unto your children: how much more shall your heavenly Father GIVE THE HOLY SPIRIT TO THEM THAT ASK HIM?
>
> Luke 11:13

One of the only things Jesus told us to pray for is the Holy Spirit. You must pray for the Holy Spirit every day! Do not think that you have enough of the Holy Spirit! Who can ever have enough of the Spirit of God?

Because the Holy Spirit has been given to us in a measure, there are always other measures that can be added to what you have. Until you die and go out of this world, you will be receiving gifts and impartations of the Holy Spirit. Each of those gifts is important for your calling. The "good thing" and the "best thing" that Jesus has for you is the Holy Spirit.

You will notice the difference in the lives and ministries of those who pray for the Holy Spirit. The most anointed people often pray for the Holy Spirit. It is when you understand and know the value of the Holy Spirit that you constantly pray for Him or His influence?. Kenneth Hagin spoke of how he prayed for the Holy Spirit for many years. Perhaps your most important prayer topic is to pray for the Holy Spirit. I love to pray for the spirit of wisdom, understanding, might, power and counsel.

Initially, I did not pray much for the Holy Spirit. I felt that I had enough of the Holy Spirit because I already spoke in tongues. Now I am constantly seeking gifts, sub-gifts and impartations. May your prayers for the Holy Spirit be answered! May you come under a greater and greater influence of the Holy Spirit through these mighty prayers!

3. Stir up the sweet influences of the Holy Spirit by having prayer meetings.

And WHEN THEY HAD PRAYED, the place was shaken where they were assembled together; and THEY WERE ALL FILLED with the Holy Ghost, and they spake the word of God with boldness.

Acts 4: 31

The book of Acts records the mighty filling of the Holy Spirit after a prayer meeting. The early church was filled with the Holy

Spirit when they prayed. They multiplied the presence of the Holy Spirit through their fervent prayer meetings.

Every prayer meeting brings down the presence of the Holy Spirit! The mention of the name of Jesus and the cries of the saints go up before the Lord as incense. You must remember that our prayers are incense rising into the throne room of God. Every prayer meeting brings us nearer the throne room of the Lord. You will be filled with the Spirit during prayer meetings.

4. Stir up the sweet influences of the Holy Spirit by speaking to yourselves in songs.

And be not drunk with wine, wherein is excess; but BE FILLED WITH THE SPIRIT;
SPEAKING TO YOURSELVES in psalms and hymns and spiritual songs, singing and making melody in your heart to the Lord;

Ephesians 5:18-19

Perhaps the most important Scripture for Christians who desire to be filled with the Spirit is Ephesians 5:18. It is the Scripture that tells us how Christians can be continually filled, empowered and influenced by the Holy Spirit. According to this landmark Scripture, the first thing you must do if you want to be filled with the Spirit is to speak to yourself through a song, a hymn or a psalm.

The key words here are *"speak to yourself"*. Think about it. Many of the songs that are sung in churches do not speak to us *because we cannot hear the words*.

Even when we can hear the words, the words do not edify or minister grace to us. If you want people to be filled with the Spirit through your music ministry, it is important that the words are powerful and that they speak to our hearts. Often, musicians put together Christian phrases, which they think are the right things to be said.

Unfortunately, joining words together or putting Christian slogans into a song does not constitute a message. *These things do not speak to us! We need something that will speak to us.* It is only someone who is close to the Lord who can speak or minister through his songs. People who do not know the Lord can only join catchphrases, rhyming words and Christian slogans together.

You must have singers who speak through their songs.

5. Stir up the sweet influences of the Holy Spirit by singing and making melody in your heart to the Lord.

And be not drunk with wine, wherein is excess; but BE FILLED WITH THE SPIRIT;

Speaking to yourselves in psalms and hymns and spiritual songs, SINGING AND MAKING MELODY IN YOUR HEART TO THE LORD;

Giving thanks always for all things unto God and the Father in the name of our Lord Jesus Christ;

Ephesians 5:18-20

Have you noticed how you feel different when you sing and make melody in your heart to the Lord? This is the reason why a time of worship has such a great impact on you. Beautiful times of worship always result in you being filled with the Spirit and coming under the sweet influences of the anointing.

It is important to create a spiritual atmosphere in your room by having music in which people sing and make melody in their hearts.

Not all Christian music has this powerful effect. Songs that are not sung from the heart do not have the same effect. The melody and the songs that result in you being filled with the Spirit must emanate from the heart.

Songs of ministers that come from their hearts and from their life's experiences, have an effect that others do not. Music that consists of rhyming words and hastily put together lyrics is not melody that comes from the heart. It is melody that is designed to impress and to make money. A spiritual person will always notice the songs that come from the heart.

6. Stir up the sweet influences of the Holy Spirit by being thankful.

And be not drunk with wine, wherein is excess; but BE FILLED WITH THE SPIRIT;

Speaking to yourselves in psalms and hymns and spiritual songs, singing and making melody in your heart to the Lord;

GIVING THANKS ALWAYS FOR ALL THINGS unto God and the Father in the name of our Lord Jesus Christ;

Ephesians 5:18-20

The next important key to being filled with the spirit and multiplying the effect of the sweet influences in your life is being thankful. "Thankfulness" causes you to be filled with the Holy Spirit. Criticism, murmuring and accusations cause you to be filled with evil sprits. You will notice that the Israelites were filled with evil spirits when they criticised Moses. Evils spirits of death, disease and destruction filled them.

Every time you are thankful and every time you praise God you open yourself to be filled with the Holy Spirit and a greater anointing.

The Scripture says you should give thanks always and for all things. It is very easy to give thanks for some things and complain about others. That is why many Christians lose the opportunity to be filled with the Spirit. They are thankful about the good things but are unable to be thankful about many other things.

Develop the habit of being thankful for everything. Develop the habit of blessing God and praising Him every day. At each turn, at each event, be thankful. It is sad that most of us are only thankful just before we eat. Thankfulness must multiply and be offered at every junction of your day.

7. Stir up the sweet influences of the Holy Spirit by being humble.

And be not drunk with wine, wherein is excess; but BE FILLED WITH THE SPIRIT;

Speaking to yourselves in psalms and hymns and spiritual songs, singing and making melody in your heart to the Lord;

Giving thanks always for all things unto God and the Father in the name of our Lord Jesus Christ;

SUBMITTING YOURSELVES ONE TO ANOTHER in the fear of God.

Ephesians 5:18-21

This is the last of the five keys that Paul enumerated in his letter to the Ephesians about being filled with the Spirit. *Be filled with the spirit, submitting yourselves one to another in the fear of God.* The last key to stirring up the sweet influences of the Holy Spirit in your life is submission and humility.

Being filled with the Holy Spirit is closely linked to "submissiveness" and humility in relation to others.

Remember that pride and arrogance are the characteristics of Lucifer or Satan. Lucifer was lifted up in pride and arrogance. He rose up against God and threatened to invade the throne of God. But he was cast down as a wretched branch.

It is therefore no surprise that submitting ourselves one to another in humility will take us far away from evil spirits and closer to the Holy Spirit.

If you do not understand how being humble and submissive helps you to be filled with the Holy Spirit, just think of submission and humility as something that takes you further away from the spirit of Satan.

CHAPTER 32

How to Catch the Anointing through "Association"

Many famous associations have stirred up the sweet influences of the Holy Spirit. Why do you have to associate with anointed men of God? What exactly do you acquire through association? As you closely associate with a man of God, you will hear him speaking over and over again. These words contain the anointing. When Elisha associated himself closely with Elijah he must have heard him speaking many times. Every kind of association has a spiritual impact.

Notice how the Scripture warns about the effects of association. Why is the Bible full of warnings about the effects of association? Because associating with someone is a deeply spiritual thing. Never take your associating with a person for granted. Every association will lead to evil or good. Because the apostles knew the effects of association, they were concerned about who their followers associated with. All Hitler's henchmen were equally full of hatred and murder. It is not easy to be associated with a satanic entity and not be affected.

I wrote you in my letter not to ASSOCIATE with immoral people;

1 Corinthians 5:9 (NASB)

But actually, I wrote to you not to ASSOCIATE with any so-called brother if he is an immoral person, or covetous, or an idolater, or a reviler, or a drunkard, or a swindler -- not even to eat with such a one.

1 Corinthians 5:11 (NASB)

a. Jesus Christ associated with His disciples.

b. Moses associated with Aaron.

c. Moses associated with Joshua.

d. Elijah associated with Elisha.

The Apostles, Peter, James and John were physically associated with the Lord Jesus. They touched him, they held him and they even had dinner with him. This is their testimony: "That which was from the beginning, which we have heard, which we have seen with our eyes, which we have looked upon, and our hands have handled..." (1 John 1:1).

Unfortunately, Apostle Paul did not have the chance to physically interact with Christ as the other apostles did. Paul was just like me; he had to depend on books! He loved his books. That is why he sent urgently for his books and parchments (booklets). He had to study and fellowship with the Lord and other great men of God like Isaiah through the written Word.

If Paul had lived in our generation he would have used all the technology available to associate even more through the written and spoken Word. Paul would have listened to CDs and watched videos. Books contain the written Word, but CDs and DVDs contain the spoken Word. You can associate with someone through his words.

Ten Things That Happen When You Associate with Someone

1. When you associate with someone you connect with the person.

2. When you associate with someone you communicate with the person.

3. When you associate with someone you flow with the person.

4. When you associate with someone you unite with the person.

5. When you associate with someone you join with the person.

6. When you associate with someone you mix with the person.

7. When you associate with someone you socialize with the person.

8. When you associate with someone you have a lot to do with the person.

9. When you associate with someone you become involved with the person.

10. When you associate with someone you relate with the person.

CHAPTER 33

How to Catch the Anointing through "Friendship"

Iron sharpeneth iron; so a man sharpeneth the countenance of his friend.

Proverbs 27:17

Many friendships have stirred up the sweet influences of the Holy Spirit. A friend is someone like you. A friend's influence on another friend is just like one iron sharpening another iron. Friendships always have a spiritual impact. You always learn from your friends. Friends have a great impact. They are silent teachers who are imparting their ways and their knowledge to you. They invade you through the heart because you are open to their ways.

> Make no FRIENDSHIP with an angry man, and with a furious man do not go, LEST YOU LEARN HIS WAYS and set a snare for your soul.
>
> Proverbs 22:24-25 (NKJV)

There is an eternal law about friendships. You become like the people you walk with. "He that walketh with wise men shall be wise ..." (Proverbs 13:20). Is it not amazing that you are becoming like your friends rather than like your pastor. You are not becoming like the man of God whose picture you have on your desk. If your best friends are motivational speakers I will not be surprised if you become a motivational speaker soon. If your best friends are anointed men of the Holy Spirit, I will not be surprised if you have a ministry like that one day.

Many friendships have stirred up the sweet influences of the Holy Spirit. We are affected more by our friends than we know. Many people are affected more by their friends than by their pastors. In a very subtle way, your friendships have a great spiritual impact on you. Most people are like their friends. Think about it! Let it soak in! Most people are not like their pastors. *Most people are like their friends!* This is why friendships are so important and this is why the anointing and the Holy Spirit will come to your life through friendships.

Ten Things That Happen When You Befriend Someone

1. When you befriend someone you *partner* with the person without even knowing.

2. When you befriend someone you *become a colleague* of the person.

3. When you befriend someone you *become one* with the person.

4. When you befriend someone you *help* the person in various ways.

5. When you befriend someone you *go around* with the person.

6. When you befriend someone you *become involved* with the person.

7. When you befriend someone you *blend* with the person.

8. When you befriend someone you *intermingle* with the person.

9. When you befriend someone you *have a deep relationship* with the person.

10. When you befriend someone you *bond* with the person.

CHAPTER 34

How to Catch the Anointing through the "Environment"

...that they might be called trees of righteousness, the planting of the Lord.

Isaiah 61:3

There are environments that stir up the sweet influences of the Holy Spirit. Have you ever wondered why apple trees do not grow in tropical West Africa? Have you ever wondered why plantain trees do not grow in England? The answer is "environment". You are God's garden and God's trees do not flourish everywhere. They need a certain environment to thrive in.

Environment is defined as the totality of surrounding conditions. Someone's environment is all the circumstances, people, things and events around him that influences his life. The environment is the area in which something exists or lives.

Many good and spiritual environments can stir up the anointing.

The miracle and spiritual environment which the disciples lived in for three years affected them greatly. John declared that he had seen, heard and felt many things which affected him.

That which was from the beginning, which WE HAVE HEARD, which we have seen with our eyes, which WE HAVE LOOKED UPON, and our hands have handled, of the Word of life;

(For the life was manifested, and WE HAVE SEEN IT, and bear witness, and shew unto you that eternal life, which was with the Father, and was manifested unto us;)

That which WE HAVE SEEN and heard declare we unto you, that ye also may have fellowship with us: and truly our fellowship is with the Father, and with his Son Jesus Christ.

1 John 1:1-3

An environment of poverty creates a certain kind of person. The poverty- stricken environment of certain places have created men who love shabbiness and are comfortable with accumulated rubbish all around them. People who grow up in other environments where old cars, old fridges, old tyres, old stoves and second-hand clothes are not displayed, have a different definition of beauty. People who grow up in an environment of real beauty and serenity inevitably create the same environment for themselves wherever they are.

The Environment That Produced Murmurers

The spiritual environment of discontentment, criticism and backbiting creates men of disloyalty and treachery. An environment creates a certain kind of person. When a person grows up in an environment of criticism, murmuring and treachery, it is not surprising that he turns out to be a Judas. That is all that he has ever known – treachery. That is all that he grew up in. That is all he will ever understand.

I once met a pastor who had grown up in a church where criticism, backbiting, slander and murmuring were the order of the day. It was not long before he manifested those exact same traits. Shortly after that, I met another person who had come out of that same environment and it was no better. Soon, I had met several pastors and Christian leaders who grew up in that environment. Every single one of them had the same traits of disloyalty and treachery. I was forced to conclude that their evil traits were a product of their environment.

What type of environment are you growing up in? The environment you are in will mysteriously affect you!

CHAPTER 35

How to Catch the Anointing through "Availability"

Association, friendship and environment expose you to men of the Holy Spirit. Through your association with these people, the influence of the Holy Spirit will increase in your life.

Being available is the master key to association, friendship and environment. Without being available, you will not have the opportunity for certain key associations, friendships and environments. People who come and go quickly, and have no time to linger around, will never develop certain associations and friendships. They will never come under the appropriate influences and never benefit from the environment.

Someone who is available is not busy. He is free to talk to you and relate with you. Most people will not pay the price to relate with an anointed person.

Availability allows you to learn, to imbibe and to assimilate the vital lessons of ministry.

Thirty Things That You Will Learn
by Being Available

1. **You will see the hidden and inner workings of ministry that the public does not see.**

   And in the morning, rising up a great while before day, he went out, and departed into a solitary place, and there prayed.

   Mark 1:35

2. **You will learn how to be a travelling minister.**

   And it came to pass, that, while Apollos was at Corinth, PAUL HAVING PASSED THROUGH THE UPPER COASTS CAME TO EPHESUS: and finding certain disciples,

   He said unto them, have ye received the Holy Ghost since ye believed? And they said unto him, we have not so much as heard whether there be any Holy Ghost.

   Acts 19:1-2

3. **You will learn how failure happens in ministry.**

   And when they were come to the multitude, there came to him a certain man, kneeling down to him, and saying, Lord, have mercy on my son: for he is lunatick, and sore vexed: for ofttimes he falleth into the fire, and oft into the water. And I brought him to thy disciples, and THEY COULD NOT CURE HIM.

   Matthew 17:14-16

4. **You will learn how to overcome failure in ministry.**

   Then came the disciples to Jesus apart, and said, why could not we cast him out? And Jesus said unto them, Because of your unbelief: for verily I say unto you, IF YE HAVE FAITH as a grain of mustard seed, ye shall say unto this mountain, Remove hence to yonder place; and it shall remove; and nothing shall be impossible unto you.

   Matthew 17:19-20

5. You will learn how to survive difficult seasons of ministry.

Thrice was I beaten with rods, once was I stoned, thrice I suffered shipwreck, a night and a day I have been in the deep;

In journeyings often, in perils of waters, in perils of robbers, in perils by mine own countrymen, in perils by the heathen, in perils in the city, in perils in the wilderness, in perils in the sea, in perils among false brethren;

In weariness and painfulness, in watchings often, in hunger and thirst, in fastings often, in cold and nakedness.

2 Corinthians 11:25-27

6. You will learn how to handle desertion in the ministry.

For Demas HATH FORSAKEN ME, having loved this present world, AND IS DEPARTED unto Thessalonica; Crescens to Galatia, Titus unto Dalmatia.

Only Luke is with me. Take Mark, and bring him with thee: for he is profitable to me for the ministry.

2 Timothy 4:10-11

At my first answer NO MAN STOOD WITH ME, but all men forsook me: I pray God that it may not be laid to their charge.

Notwithstanding the Lord stood with me, and strengthened me; that by me the preaching might be fully known, and that all the Gentiles might hear: and I was delivered out of the mouth of the lion.

2 Timothy 4:16-17

7. You will learn how to deal with wicked people in the ministry.

The cloke that I left at Troas with Carpus, when thou comest, bring with thee, and the books, but especially the parchments.

Alexander the coppersmith did me much evil: the Lord reward him according to his works: Of whom be thou ware also; for he hath greatly withstood our words.

2 Timothy 4:13-15

8. You will learn about hunger and fasting.

In weariness and painfulness, in watchings often, IN HUNGER AND THIRST, in fastings often, in cold and nakedness.

2 Corinthians 11:27

9. You will learn about how to conduct outreaches in resistant communities.

And he went into the synagogue, and spake boldly for the space of three months, disputing and persuading the things concerning the kingdom of God.

But when DIVERS WERE HARDENED, and believed not, but spake evil of that way before the multitude, he departed from them, and separated the disciples, disputing daily in the school of one Tyrannus.

Acts 19:8-9

10. You will learn about different types of prayer.

Then they took away the stone from the place where the dead was laid. And Jesus lifted up his eyes, and said, Father, I thank thee that thou hast heard me.

And I knew that thou hearest me always: but because of the people which stand by I said it, that they may believe that thou hast sent me.

John 11:41-42

11. You will learn how to apologise.

And the high priest Ananias commanded them that stood by him to smite him on the mouth.

Then said Paul unto him, God shall smite thee, thou whited wall: for sittest thou to judge me after the law, and commandest me to be smitten contrary to the law?

And they that stood by said, Revilest thou God's high priest?

THEN SAID PAUL, I WIST NOT, BRETHREN, that he was the high priest: for it is written, Thou shalt not speak evil of the ruler of thy people.

Acts 23:2-5

12. You will learn how to do menial jobs.

When they were filled, he said unto his disciples, GATHER UP THE FRAGMENTS that remain, that nothing be lost.

Therefore they gathered them together, and filled twelve baskets with the fragments of the five barley loaves, which remained over and above unto them that had eaten.

John 6:12-13

13. You will receive the anointing.

Then said Jesus to them again, Peace be unto you: as my Father hath sent me, even so send I you. And when he had said this, he breathed on them, and saith unto them, RECEIVE YE THE HOLY GHOST.

John 20:21-22

14. You will assimilate the spirit of the ministry.

And sent messengers before his face: and they went, and entered into a village of the Samaritans, to make ready for him.

And they did not receive him, because his face was as though he would go to Jerusalem.

And when his disciples James and John saw this, they said, Lord, wilt thou that we command fire to come down from heaven, and consume them, even as Elias did?

But he turned, and rebuked them, and said, YE KNOW NOT WHAT MANNER OF SPIRIT YE ARE OF.

Luke 9:52-55

15. You will learn how to counsel people.

There cometh a woman of Samaria to draw water: JESUS SAITH UNTO HER, give me to drink. (For his disciples were gone away unto the city to buy meat.)

Then saith the woman of Samaria unto him, how is it that thou, being a Jew, askest drink of me, which am a woman of Samaria? For the Jews have no dealings with the Samaritans.

Jesus answered and said unto her, If thou knewest the gift of God, and who it is that saith to thee, Give me to drink; thou wouldest have asked of him, and he would have given thee living water.

John 4:7-10

16. You will learn how to handle difficult cases.

And he cometh to Bethsaida; and they bring a blind man unto him, and besought him to touch him.

And he took the blind man by the hand, and led him out of the town; and when he had spit on his eyes, and put his hands upon him, he asked him if he saw ought.

And he looked up, and said, I SEE MEN AS TREES, walking.

After that he put his hands again upon his eyes, and made him look up: and he was restored, and saw every man clearly.

Mark 8:22-25

17. You will learn to be focused in the ministry.

And when they saw it, they all murmured, saying, that he was gone to be guest with a man that is a sinner.

And Zacchaeus stood, and said unto the Lord; Behold, Lord, the half of my goods I give to the poor; and if I have

122

taken any thing from any man by false accusation, I restore him fourfold.

And Jesus said unto him, this day is salvation come to this house, forsomuch as he also is a son of Abraham.

For the SON OF MAN IS COME TO SEEK AND TO SAVE that which was lost.

Luke 19:7-10

18. You will learn about safety procedures in ministry.

TAKE HEED UNTO THYSELF, and unto the doctrine; continue in them: for in doing this thou shalt both save thyself, and them that hear thee.

1 Timothy 4:16

19. You will learn how to see the evil ahead.

And said unto them, SIRS, I PERCEIVE THAT THIS VOYAGE WILL BE WITH HURT and much damage, not only of the lading and ship, but also of our lives.

Acts 27:10

20. You will learn about the risks of ministry.

But as they sailed he fell asleep: and there came down a storm of wind on the lake; and THEY WERE FILLED WITH WATER, and were in jeopardy.

Luke 8:23

21. You will develop close relationships.

And it was told him by certain which said, Thy mother and thy brethren stand without, desiring to see thee.

And he answered and said unto them, My mother and MY BRETHREN ARE THESE which hear the word of God, and do it.

Luke 8:20-21

22. You will hear about great secrets and listen to mystical things.

Then HE TOOK UNTO HIM THE TWELVE, AND SAID UNTO THEM, Behold, we go up to Jerusalem, and all things that are written by the prophets concerning the Son of man shall be accomplished.

For he shall be delivered unto the Gentiles, and shall be mocked, and spitefully entreated, and spitted on: And they shall scourge him, and put him to death: and the third day he shall rise again.

And they understood none of these things: and this saying was hid from them, neither knew they the things which were spoken.

Luke 18:31-34

23. You will learn about how to be a servant.

But Jehoshaphat said, is there not here a prophet of the Lord, that we may enquire of the Lord by him? And one of the king of Israel's servants answered and said, here is Elisha the son of Shaphat, WHICH POURED WATER ON THE HANDS OF ELIJAH.

2 Kings 3:11

24. You will learn about how to hear the voice of God.

Therefore Eli said unto Samuel, Go, lie down: and it shall be, if he call thee, that THOU SHALT SAY, SPEAK, Lord; for thy servant heareth. So Samuel went and lay down in his place.

And the Lord came, and stood, and called as at other times, Samuel, Samuel. Then Samuel answered, Speak; for thy servant heareth.

1 Samuel 3:9-10

25. You will learn how to work for long hours.

And upon the first day of the week, when the disciples came together to break bread, PAUL PREACHED UNTO

THEM, ready to depart on the morrow; and continued his speech UNTIL MIDNIGHT.

Acts 20:7

26. You will learn about how to wait patiently for your leader.

And he cometh unto the disciples, and findeth them asleep, and saith unto Peter, What, COULD YE NOT WATCH WITH ME ONE HOUR?

Watch and pray, that ye enter not into temptation: the spirit indeed is willing, but the flesh is weak.

He went away again the second time, and prayed, saying, O my Father, if this cup may not pass away from me, except I drink it, thy will be done.

And he came and found them asleep again: for their eyes were heavy.

And he left them, and went away again, and prayed the third time, saying the same words.

Matthew 26:40-44

27. You will have spiritual experiences that are important for your total spiritual development.

And after six days Jesus taketh Peter, James, and John his brother, and BRINGETH THEM UP INTO AN HIGH MOUNTAIN APART, And was transfigured before them: and his face did shine as the sun, and his raiment was white as the light.

And, behold, there appeared unto them Moses and Elias talking with him.

Then answered Peter, and said unto Jesus, Lord, it is good for us to be here: if thou wilt, let us make here three tabernacles; one for thee, and one for Moses, and one for Elias.

While he yet spake, behold, a bright cloud overshadowed them: and behold a voice out of the cloud, which said, This is my beloved Son, in whom I am well pleased; hear ye him.

125

And when the disciples heard it, they fell on their face, and were sore afraid.

Matthew 17:1-6

28. You will learn how and when to minister the Spirit.

And he said unto them, unto what then were ye baptized? And they said, Unto John's baptism.

Then said Paul, John verily baptized with the baptism of repentance, saying unto the people, that they should believe on him which should come after him, that is, on Christ Jesus.

When they heard this, they were baptized in the name of the Lord Jesus.

And when PAUL HAD LAID HIS HANDS upon them, the Holy Ghost came on them; and they spake with tongues, and prophesied.

Acts 19:3-6

29. You will learn how and when to minister healing.

And there sat a certain man at Lystra, impotent in his feet, being a cripple from his mother's womb, who never had walked:

The same heard Paul speak: who stedfastly beholding him, and PERCEIVING THAT HE HAD FAITH TO BE HEALED,

Said with a loud voice, stand upright on thy feet. And he leaped and walked.

Acts 14:8-10

30. [77]You will learn how to relate to those who were in the ministry before you.

Then after three years I went up to Jerusalem to see Peter, and abode with him fifteen days.

Galatians 1:18